NOVEL TAKES

ESSAYS ON LITERATURE

by

GREG JOHNSON

Counter-Currents Publishing Ltd.
San Francisco
2024

Copyright © 2024 by Greg Johnson
All rights reserved

Cover image by
Jean Jacques Lagrenée,
St. Jerome in a Landscape, 1762–1763

Cover design by
Kevin I. Slaughter

Published in the United States by
COUNTER-CURRENTS PUBLISHING LTD.
http://www.counter-currents.com/

Hardcover ISBN: 978-1-64264-047-2
Paperback ISBN: 978-1-64264-048-9
E-book ISBN: 978-1-64264-049-6

Contents

Preface ❖ iii

Dystopian Visions
1. Jean Raspail's *The Camp of the Saints* ❖ 1
2. H. P. Lovecraft's *The Shadow over Innsmouth* ❖ 13
3. Philip K. Dick's *Do Androids Dream of Electric Sheep?* as Anti-Semitic/Christian-Gnostic Allegory ❖ 21
4. Michel Houllebecq's *Submission* ❖ 30
5. A Farewell to Reason: Michel Houllebecq's *Annihilation* ❖ 42

Frank Herbert
6. Frank Herbert: Our Prophet ❖ 54
7. Archeofuturist Fiction: Frank Herbert's *Dune* ❖ 63
8. Notes on *Dune Messiah* ❖ 69
9. The Golden Path: Frank Herbert's *Children of Dune & God Emperor of Dune* ❖ 74
10. The Bene Gesserit Books: Frank Herbert's *Heretics of Dune & Chapterhouse Dune* ❖ 88

Tito Perdue
11. Waiting for Saint Benedict: Tito Perdue's *Morning Crafts* ❖ 101
12. Turning the World Around: Tito Perdue's *The Node* ❖ 108
13. The Cultured Thug: Tito Perdue's *Reuben* ❖ 113

Cautionary Tales
14. John Kennedy Toole's *A Confederacy of Dunces* ❖ 123
15. Bill Hopkins' *The Leap!* ❖ 135

Engaged Literature
16. Superheroes, Sovereignty, & the Deep State ❖ 146

17. Birth of a Nation: H. A. Covington's Northwest Quartet ❖ 158
18. Farnham O'Reilly's *Hyperborean Home* ❖ 176
19. Notes on Chuck Palahniuk's *Adjustment Day* ❖ 183
20. Ayn Rand's *Ideal: The Novel & the Play* ❖ 188
21. The Meaning of Mishima's Death ❖ 196

Index ❖ 201

About the Author ❖ 218

Preface

There's a lot more truth to be found in fiction than nonfiction. But I stubbornly remain focused on the latter. Occasionally, though, I write something on fiction, but my focus has been primarily on film criticism (five volumes so far). This book is my first to focus on literature. It collects twenty-one essays, lectures, and reviews written between 2009 and 2024.[1]

The title, *Novel Takes*, has two meanings. First, these essays deal with novels, novellas, novelists, and the superhero genre which spills across multiple media, including novels. Second, I like to think that I have novel things to say about them.

My approach to reading fiction is straightforward and naïve. I write because I have something to say. I assume that other writers have the same motive. I read them to learn what they have to say. I write about other authors to covey their messages to you, my readers.

Of course no commentary is a substitute for the original. My aim is to deepen your appreciation of texts you have already read or to introduce you to works you may want to read.

Because these texts were written over a long period of time, I occasionally repeat myself. I may even contradict

---

[1] Twenty of these pieces were first published at *Counter-Currents*. One other, "Birth of a Nation: H. A. Covington's Northwest Quartet," first appeared at *The Occidental Quarterly*. Two of these essays have already appeared in other collections: the Covington essay in *In Defense of Prejudice* (San Francisco: Counter-Currents, 2017) and "Superheroes, Sovereignty, and the Deep State" in the first edition of *Toward a New Nationalism* (San Francisco: Counter-Currents, 2019). It was dropped from the second edition. I included both pieces here for completeness.

myself. But I hope that whatever virtues you find here will persuade you to overlook such flaws.

I wish to thank James O'Meara, David Zsutty, and Jef Costello for helping to edit and proof this collection; James O'Meara for preparing the Index; Jef Costello, James O'Meara, and Tito Perdue for their promotional quotes; Kevin Slaughter for creating the cover; and the many writers, donors, and commenters at *Counter-Currents* who make all my work possible.

It is only appropriate that I dedicate this book to Tito Perdue, who is not just a great novelist but also a great friend.

November 16, 2024

Jean Raspail's
The Camp of the Saints

Whenever someone says, "We need a great White Nationalist novel," I hand them *The Camp of the Saints*, for as a depiction of white dispossession and a call to racial awareness, Jean Raspail's 1973 masterpiece has never been equaled or bettered.

The Camp of the Saints is a beautifully written book, filled with aphoristic turns of phrase worthy of Nietzsche. The narrative is gripping. The characters are vividly drawn and feel real. But I don't want to linger over its literary qualities. I will let you discover those pleasures on your own. Instead, I want to focus on its message.

The Camp of the Saints is obviously a dystopian novel. The purpose of every dystopian novel is to be wrong. Such books are warnings. If they are successful warnings later generations can smugly dismiss them as mistaken. Raspail went to his grave in 2020, at the age of 94, with the gnawing feeling that he had been right. *The Camp of the Saints* was written as a prophecy, but with each passing year, it reads more like the daily news.

The Camp of the Saints also belongs to another genre: the murder mystery. The victim is the white race. But Raspail leaves it to us to unravel the identity of the killers and figure out how the crime was committed. If we can do so, maybe we can halt the same crime that is happening to our race today.

Initially, *The Camp of the Saints* is depressing, but its overall effect is to raise your fighting spirit. Still, a fighting spirit means nothing unless you can direct it intelligently. Raspail has much to teach us here. Distilling those lessons is the purpose of this essay.

Here's the basic story: there is famine in India. About a

million starving refugees under the leadership of a massive Hindu known as the "turd eater" and his misshapen dwarf son head for Europe by commandeering a fleet of rusting ships.

In Europe all the leading voices of the churches, the political Left, and the Leftist-dominated establishment frenziedly extend a welcome in the name of human brotherhood, white guilt, and the absurd idea that we get richer by sharing everything with beggars. But perhaps we deserve it for our sins.

As the fleet draws closer, more and more whites have reservations. But they do nothing to stop the migration because they are cowed by the media, the churches, and their own consciences, which have been shaped by nearly 2000 years of Christianity, several centuries of liberal humanism, and several decades of Marxist propaganda.

Nonwhites around the world, and especially in white countries, are also watching the unfolding drama with great excitement, growing bolder as white altruism reaches a crescendo and white resistance fails to materialize.

Of course, political leaders realized that you can't just invite in a million starving beggars who differ profoundly in race, language, religion, and culture without disaster. All it would take is a simple misunderstanding to ignite a race war. Even in the best-case scenario, it would be impossible to feed, house, and educate them at a First-World level. They would quickly overwhelm society and bring it down to their level. These people are the refuse of India, not their best. Theft and murder would run amok. Starving people also bring epidemics.

Beyond that, it won't stop with one fleet; if one fleet is welcomed, others will follow.

Allowing them to set out was a folly. They should have been promptly turned back. But no one would take responsibility for such a decision. They were too afraid of bad press and the scoldings of priests and women.

Besides, when the fleet set out, it could have ended up anywhere, including at the bottom of the sea. Why would any political leader risk bad press warding off what will probably be other people's problems?

When the fleet neared Europe, it should have been sunk. Yes, it would be a terrible loss of life—which India could, by the way, replace in a matter of days—but it would have prevented even worse horrors. Yet no one would take responsibility for such a decision, lest they be pilloried in the press and tried as criminals. And, again, why risk anything when the fleet might still be somebody else's problem?

When the migrants arrived in Europe, they should not have been allowed to disembark freely. Instead, they should have been interned in remote camps to shield the native population from disease and crime. Yet no one would take responsibility for such a decision, for it would trigger neurotics by reminding them of the Nazis.

As the fleet entered the Mediterranean, Spain braced itself for invasion. But the fleet sailed on by, although they left behind a horrifying memento: the corpses of whites and Asians who had embarked with them. The Indians were rejecting all diversity and hardening themselves into a unified invasion force as they prepared to land in Europe. The fist was closing. Obviously a blow would fall. At this point there was no excuse not to treat the fleet as hostile and repel it with force.

When the fleet approached the French coast, trust in the system evaporated, and millions fled. While their lips paid homage to universal brotherhood, their feet carried them to safety. All of them asked, "Why won't *other people* take a stand to protect our lives and property and civilization itself—and, of course, allow the Left to martyr them for doing the right thing?"

The measure of "progress" is the extent to which people can assume that virtue will not merely go unrewarded but will actively be punished—the extent to which they can assume that their neighbors will act from fear and selfishness rather than decency and solidarity. Such a society collapses at the first blow.

The white refugees were met along the way by a flood of people moving south to welcome the invaders: priests, hippies, motorcycle gangsters, escaped convicts, madmen, journalists . . . The traitors' motives were a brew of ideology, egomania, hatred of their own, and nihilism. They expected to be greeted as saviors and rewarded as turncoats. But although some were raped and others were murdered, most were just brushed aside by the Ganges migrants as irrelevant. None of them got what they wanted, except those who wanted pure destruction.

Once the fleet landed and France descended into chaos, the government was overthrown by a Leftist junta. The new government then used the French military to suppress the resistance of the native French. France was finished as a white society. It became legal to rob Frenchmen and to rape French women.

Millions more Third Worlders swarmed into other European societies, which shared the same fate as France. The last holdout was Switzerland, where the chronicle we are reading has been written. But it too, like South Africa and Rhodesia, has finally succumbed to international pressure.

If whites do not find the will to stem the tide, future historians, no doubt Chinese, will debate why the white race allowed itself to be extinguished. Throughout the book, Raspail invites us to consider different explanations.

Why, on Raspail's account, is the white race facing extermination? He doesn't think it is a ghastly misunderstanding. He doesn't think it is the accidental convergence of different forces. He thinks it is the product of conscious planning on the part of non-whites who hate whites and wish us to perish. If there is an element of accident or coincidence, it is only the meshing together of many independent anti-white conspiracies.

Why are we hated to the point of genocide? It is complicated, but whites are not just hated for our crimes, real and imagined, but also for our virtues. The beauty of our race and our creations; the power of our science, technologies, and armies; our wealthy, free, and orderly societies: all of these inevitably stir feelings of resentment and envy, the desire to take what we have—or, barring that, to make us lose it.

But this sort of evil has always existed. Surely, if we are powerful enough to stir such envy, we are also powerful enough to resist it. So how did the white man become a colossus with feet of clay? Why are we enabling our own genocide? The answer is a spiritual weakness that Raspail attributes primarily to Christianity and its moral offshoots, including secular liberalism and Leftism.

For convenience, I will call this spiritual weakness "white guilt." White guilt means that whites are somehow responsible for the suffering of non-whites all over the world. To atone for this guilt, we must suffer in turn. We must give up everything that non-whites lack.

Christianity is the root of white guilt, because it teaches that humans can be collectively guilty for things that other people have done. Christianity undermines nationalism, ethnocentrism, and racism by proclaiming the brotherhood of mankind, thereby expanding our moral community and our moral obligations to the ends of the Earth. Christianity also inverts the natural order of values, preaching that those who lack are better than those who have. Want to overthrow society? Just make weakness sacred. Finally, Christianity preaches magical redemption by the imitation of Christ, namely suffering and self-sacrifice by the haves for the have-nots. Without nearly 2000 years of Christianity shaping white minds, the basic elements of white guilt would never have been plausible.

Raspail seems to be of two minds about Christianity. On the one hand, it is the major source of the moral rot that is destroying the West. Christians, especially clergy, are prominent among the worst traitors and the most useless defenders of the West. On the other hand, he regards Christianity as part of French history and identity and looks back with nostalgia on the times when its most destructive influences were held in check.

Christianity may provide all the necessary conditions for complete racial nihilism, but it also contains two ideas that block its full realization. First is the universality of original sin. If you take Christianity seriously, non-whites and their champions are no less depraved than white colonists and oppressors. Second, the final reckoning with evil is God's work, which is deferred to the end of the world.

Secular liberal humanitarianism does away with both of these *katechons*. Original sin is replaced by the natural goodness of mankind, which allows us to believe that the more primitive or immature (viz., "natural") a person is, the more innocent he is. It also allows the champions of the downtrodden to feel entirely righteous in prosecuting their cause. The removal of the final judgment allows the self-annointed and self-righteous to believe that they can conquer evil and return mankind to innocence within history. These views lead straight to the Left's strange blend of sentimentalism and savagery.

Intellectually speaking, Marxism adds almost nothing to liberal humanitarianism, save perhaps the idea that white saviors should not be the only agents of global justice. Non-whites too should work for their own liberation, primarily through crime and parasitism, which whites should accept because we deserve it for our sins. But in terms of political organization, no force on Earth was better than Marxism at unleashing savagery and destruction.

During the Cold War, however, Marxism went underground in the West, penetrating educational, cultural, charitable, and political institutions and promoting the inclusion and upward mobility of "marginalized" groups: women, sexual minorities, and especially non-whites.

Raspail is masterful at chronicling how a network of churches and secular charities (what we today call "Non-Governmental Organizations," or NGOs) worked to move non-whites into Europe by such means as promoting adoptions. The NGOs were also there to facilitate the sailing of the flotilla, even though it was an act of mass piracy.

Once the fleet was launched, the presses and pulpits of the white world sprang into action to welcome them and browbeat any resistance. One day, every child in every elementary school in France was made to write a report on the poor migrants and why they should be welcomed. The rest of the education system also promoted the same message in lock-step. Politicians, prelates, celebrities, and Nobel laureates competed with one another to get the most screen time and deliver the most fulsome welcomes. Perhaps the most nauseating claim was that the boatloads of emaciated Hindus were more than a million Christs coming to redeem the West from the sins of racism, colonialism, and cleanliness.

Readers of the *The Camp of the Saints* found the "Migrant Crisis" of 2015 eerily foreshadowed.

But, as the flotilla neared France, millions of people along the coast—probably almost every actual Frenchman—chose to flee. Most Frenchmen did not wish to destroy their nation, their civilization, and their people.

So how did it happen? If they simply refused to let it happen, it would not have happened. So why didn't they refuse? Because they were of two minds about their survival. On the one hand, they desired to keep their own lives, families, property, homeland, and future. On the other hand, they felt that this was selfish, because non-whites have less, so their claim was stronger.

It was easy to profess such altruistic views toward non-whites when there was little danger of having to live by them. In fact, in modern society, professing racial altruism is in one's self-interest. It is so lavishly rewarded that people compete to write ever larger checks that society can never cash.

When, however, the time to pay up loomed, three groups emerged. The first group consisted of those who believed in white guilt and would follow the logic of their ideas into the abyss. These were the people who rushed to the coast. The second and largest group consisted of those who rejected white guilt, or at least rejected its most destructive consequences, but feared to do so openly. These were the people who fled. The third and smallest group consisted of those who openly rejected white guilt root and branch. These were the people who fought, until the French government sent the military to destroy them—while turning a blind eye to murder, rape, and general delinquency, as long as they were committed by non-whites.

Readers of *The Camp of the Saints* find the two-tier, anti-white justice systems in Western countries quite familiar.

Why did the Leftist minority triumph over the vast majority? Because the Left was organized, the Right was impotent, and the vast majority lacked leadership. They were a panicked rabble, each looking out for himself. Such a rabble can only coalesce into a unified force if a figure with recognized leadership skills takes a stand and demands that others do so as well.

A well-meaning nobody can't do it, because people will look at him and think, "I might follow him, but others won't, and if others won't, then I will step out of the crowd and be exposed and vulnerable. Better to just stay in the crowd." It is safer as an individual. But if every individual does the same, then none of them are safe. They are all counting on *someone else* to save them, *someone else* to be brave, so they don't have to.

But modern society does not breed and elevate natural leaders. Instead, it elevates celebrities. But nobody will follow pop stars, actors, or football players into battle.

How did the Left gain so much power? Basically, because the Right—the natural guardians of order—gave it away. The Right fell into the hands of unserious, anti-intellectual men who thought that power lies in arms and money, not in the ideas that guide their use. But, as the French discovered in *The Camp of the Saints*, their military was of no use when their men were too demoralized and mutinous to repel an unarmed invasion of starving beggars.

The Right foolishly allowed the Left to take over religious, cultural, and educational institutions as platforms to preach white guilt. To the Right, such ideas seemed at best high-minded and impracticable, at worst stupid, crazy, and evil. But never for a minute did they take them *seriously* and think that they might *matter* someday.

But what about intellectuals of the Right? Surely some men of the Right understood the importance of ideas and the true goals of the Left. Surely someone understood the magnitude of the crisis and what was necessary to avert it. Such men exist in *The Camp of the Saints*, just as they exist today. But in the novel, as in today's world, such voices are marginalized and impoverished: driven out of academia, the churches, and the mainstream media and forced to beg for subsistence from equally marginalized patrons.

In *The Camp of the Saints*, the Right-wing intellectual is Jules Machefer, publisher of *La Pensée Nationale*, a tiny, ill-funded daily paper. As the migrant fleet approaches, the president of the republic himself tries to get Machefer to speak out. Yes, even the president—who could unleash nuclear weapons, if he so wished—is desperate for *someone else* to be brave so he doesn't have to, an attitude that should immediately impeach any political leader. Large cash donations suddenly appear. But Machefer is too embittered and pessimistic to act. He thinks it is too little, too late. Maybe it is.

What could have halted this disaster, saving France and ultimately the whole white world? A leader brave and ruthless enough to do whatever it took to stop the fleet. The sooner the better. Simply sending warships to escort the fleet back to India would have prevented the crisis with little or no loss of life. The only cost would be enduring some squawking from priests and journalists.

When the fleet entered the Mediterranean, it was already clear that it was a hostile invasion force. It should simply have been sunk. If the military mutinied, the mutineers should have been stood against the wall and shot until the survivors complied. Interestingly, Raspail says nothing about mutiny when the Left orders the military to suppress the resistance of the native French. But the Left has leaders. The Right does not.

"World opinion," of course, would execrate anyone who stopped the fleet. But in secret, most people would have been relieved. Democracy means giving the people what they really want, and when they are too weak or stupid to choose it for themselves, it sometimes takes a dictator to enact the people's will. This is why most societies have constitutional measures to grant the chief executive broad emergency powers as well as immunity from prosecution for using them. Using such powers is simply a matter of will, which the Left has and the Right lacks. But will needs a moral sanction, which the ideology of white guilt denies.

What if an ungrateful world wishes to martyr the man who saved it? It would not be the first time. But whoever said that heroism was easy? Every soldier and statesman should be willing to lay down his life for the salvation of his people.

Again, this is ultimately a question of moral character. But modern society does not breed such men. Thus, the appearance of such a leader is basically a *deus ex machina*, a miracle, and no serious society should depend on miracles to survive. So it is worth asking: how could we prevent such a crisis from taking place to begin with?

Raspail is right: the ultimate cause of the crisis is moral. Thus it must be fought primarily on moral grounds. If we are to overthrow the false premises of white guilt, then we must defend these ideas instead:

- ❖ White people do not bear collective guilt for the acts of others. But collective pride in our race and nations is perfectly healthy and moral.
- ❖ We have obligations to other human beings. But our obligations to others are not equal. We owe more to people who are biologically and culturally close to us than to those who are biologically and culturally remote. Preferences for one's own are natural, normal, and right. The political system most consistent with human biological and cultural diversity, as well as in-group preferences, is nationalism for all nations, a world with borders.
- ❖ The classical rather than the Christian scale of values is correct. Merit is based on virtue, not need; strength, not weakness.
- ❖ We are not magically redeemed from fake guilt through suffering and self-sacrifice.
- ❖ Human beings are not naturally good or innocent. Human goodness is rare and requires cultivation. Nobody attains virtue merely by professing the right ideas or championing the people who lack.
- ❖ Suffering and weakness do not entitle you to victimize others.

If these views are widely accepted, white guilt will simply be inconceivable. But this is an immense task. Our enemies have a 2000-year head start. But that's just an argument for getting started right away.

To overthrow white guilt is to elevate white pride and self-assertion in its place. A pro-white moral revolution would make a political revolution unnecessary. If white identity and interests become sacrosanct, then we need not tear down old institutions or found new ones. Instead, all existing institutions would simply become pro-white—universities, churches, the media, and every political party, Right, Left, and center—just as today all of these institutions are anti-white.

Of course, pursuing a long-term metapolitical strategy does not prevent us from seizing whatever political gains might present themselves in the short term. We must, of course, close our borders, eliminate all laws and treaties that promote migration, then begin mass remigration of non-whites. Moreover, whenever possible, the Right must destroy the institutions of the Left and replace them with pro-white institutions. Anti-white organizations must be shut down. Anti-whites must be purged from academia, the media, and all branches of government, and pro-whites must be put in their places. Churches should lose their tax-exempt status if they don't crack down on Leftist clergy. They need to be reminded that their kingdom is not of this world.

Archimedes once said that if he had a lever and a place to stand, he could move the entire world. That's our goal: nothing less than to change the course of world history. Our lever is pro-white ideas. The place we stand is our movement and its institutions. In the last half-century, both awareness of our ideas and the size and power of our movement have grown enormously, in part because of *The Camp of the Saints*. When white people win back our future, we will owe a great debt to Jean Raspail.

Counter-Currents, November 29, 2024

H. P. LOVECRAFT'S
THE SHADOW OVER INNSMOUTH[*]

H. P. Lovecraft's novella *The Shadow Over Innsmouth*, written in 1931 and published in 1936, is set in an isolated Massachusetts seaport called Innsmouth and tells the story of the creation of a community of racial hybrids: human beings who have become interbred with the "Deep Ones," an immeasurably ancient and long-lived amphibious race with fishlike and froglike features.

The novel also tells of the discovery and exposure of the community by an unnamed traveler whose love of architecture and skeptical-minded materialism are based on Lovecraft himself. The novel ends with the narrator's subsequent discovery of the same biological taint in his own lineage.

The Shadow over Innsmouth is one of Lovecraft's most suspenseful and atmospheric tales. It is also unusually action-oriented. The style is relatively straightforward, although there are touches of Lovecraft's delightful overwriting. *Shadow* is also one of Lovecraft's most explicitly racialist and xenophobic tales, which has not escaped the attention of readers and critics. But I also wish to argue that it can be read as an allegory about specifically Jewish forms of subversion and how Lovecraft thought they might be remedied.

The Shadow Over Innsmouth is divided into five chapters and has a complex narrative structure. There are three nested stories. The first story is the outermost narrative framework, told at the beginning of chapter 1 and

---

[*] This essay is based on a talk delivered in honor of H. P. Lovecraft's birthday (August 20, 1890) at a Counter-Currents gathering in New York City on August 16, 2015.

in chapter 5, which is set in the narrator's present sometime in the early 1930s. The second story is set on July 15–16, 1927 and takes up chapters 2 and 4. It tells of the narrator's visit to Innsmouth, where he discovers a monstrous secret and is forced to flee for his life. The third story, which takes up most of chapter 3, is told by Innsmouth resident Zadok Allen, a "half-crazed liquorish nonagenarian,"[1] who reveals how the town was infiltrated and taken over by the Deep Ones.

Our narrator hails from Ohio. He was celebrating his coming of age with a tour of New England, during which he was pursuing genealogical and antiquarian researches. He planned to set out on July 15th from Newburyport to Arkham, from which his mother's family hailed. To save money on a train ticket, he decided to take a bus through the hitherto unknown town of Innsmouth.

Innsmouth, he quickly discovered, had an evil reputation in the neighboring towns. Innsmouth was founded in 1643 and grew into a large and prosperous seaport, but it was almost deserted at present. In the early 19th century, the economy fell on hard times, and half the population had been killed by an epidemic in 1846. The remaining Innsmouth folk numbered between 300 and 400.

They had reputation for some sort of racial miscegenation or biological degeneration, which gave rise to a distinctive "Innsmouth look" that evoked revulsion in men and beasts alike. The railroad station agent in Newburyport frankly referred to this revulsion as "race prejudice" (p. 591) but made no apology for it and indeed admitted that he shared it himself. The Innsmouth residents, moreover, had a reputation for being "lawless and sly, and full of secret doings" (p. 593). Strangers were

---

[1] H. P. Lovecraft, *The Shadow Over Innsmouth*, in *Tales*, ed. Peter Straub (New York: The Library of America, 2005), pp. 610–11.

unwelcome, and more than a few prying outsiders had gone missing over the years.

His curiosity piqued, the narrator spent the afternoon and evening of the 14th doing research on Innsmouth. He decided to take the next morning's bus to Innsmouth, spend the afternoon exploring the town, and then take the evening bus to Arkham.

Our narrator found Innsmouth to be largely deserted and in a state of advanced decay. Most buildings were empty and boarded up, with peeling paint and sagging roofs. Even the inhabited ones were in disrepair, except for the mansions of the remaining wealthy families. There were few businesses and little industry except for fishing and the Marsh gold refinery. There were no domestic animals in the town—cats, dogs, or horses—because they instinctively disliked the Innsmouth folk. The whole town was pervaded by a sickening fishy stench.

According to Zadok Allen, Innsmouth's decay was ultimately due to the subversion and replacement of the original population by an alien group. It began in the 1820s and 1830s, when Captain Obed Marsh ran three ships out of Innsmouth that traded in the East Indies. There Marsh discovered an Island of "Kanakys"—a term for the Australoid peoples of Melanesia—who enjoyed bountiful catches and an abundance of gold due to traffic with a mysterious and ancient race of amphibious creatures, the Deep Ones, whom the Kanakys worshiped as gods.

At first, Marsh only dealt with the Deep Ones through the Kanakys, bringing home rich cargoes of golden ornaments which he melted down, reviving Innsmouth's flagging economy. But in 1838, Marsh discovered that the Kanakys had been massacred by neighboring islanders. However, their chief had told Captain Marsh how he could contact the Deep Ones who dwelled beneath Devil Reef outside of Innsmouth harbor, so he entered into direct commerce with a local community of Deep Ones.

Despite their wide geographical separation, the communities of Deep Ones subverted and controlled both the Kanakys and people of Innsmouth using the same techniques.

First, the Deep Ones offered concrete worldly benefits—good fishing and golden trinkets—in exchange for worship and human sacrifices. This appealed to Captain Marsh, who as a hard-headed Yankee pragmatist, saw no value in Christianity, which promised only otherworldly rewards in exchange for enduring rather than changing this world.

This parallels the Jewish strategy of using commerce, especially money-lending, to gain influence over gentile societies. It also parallels the this-worldly orientation of the Jewish religion. There is a somewhat fainter analogy to the influence Jews exercise over Christianity as their "elder brothers in faith," which leads some Christian sects to virtually worship Jews as gods on Earth.

Second, the Deep Ones invited themselves ashore to mingle with humans, particularly on their two great festivals, Walpurgisnacht (April 30th) and Halloween (October 31st). The Kanakys and Innsmouthites had become too dependent on their commerce with the Deep Ones to say no. In Innsmouth, the Deep Ones founded a secret initiatic society, the Esoteric Order of Dagon, to instruct the natives in their new religion. The Order spread rapidly, replacing Freemasonry entirely and hollowing out and taking over the Christian churches. Those who opposed the Order mysteriously disappeared.

This parallels the Jewish strategy of seeking to control the opinion-shaping institutions of gentile societies—churches and fraternal orders, the educational system, the mass media, etc.—to secure and promote Jewish interests.

Third, the Deep Ones then offered their daughters in marriage to prominent men in the human communities, promising that the offspring of such unions, who carried the Deep Ones' blood, would start their lives as humans, thus giving the Deep Ones a foothold and cover on dry land. But, as they aged, they would change slowly into Deep Ones, eventually taking to the seas, where they would enjoy bodily immortality, for—barring accident or violence—the Deep Ones never die.

This parallels the widespread Jewish practice of marrying (or whoring) out their women to prominent gentiles, which extends Jewish influence, as illustrated by the myth of Queen Esther. The dogma of the matrilineal descent of Jewish identity leads the offspring of such matches to think of themselves as Jews and promote the interests of the Jewish community. Lovecraft himself married a Jewish woman, Sonia Greene, in 1924, but they separated soon after and the marriage was without issue. The physical immortality of the Deep Ones also parallels the Jewish and Christian idea of physical immortality in a resurrected body rather than the Indo-European idea of the spiritual immortality of a separated soul.

Finally, in 1846, after eight years of subversion, an organized opposition grew up in Innsmouth. Captain Marsh and his collaborators were arrested, but before they could be prosecuted, the Deep Ones rose up in number, massacred half the town, and subjugated the rest with terror, oaths, bribes, and brides. The outside world was told that an epidemic had struck, which explained away the murders and scared away the neighbors. Having gained complete control of Innsmouth, the Deep Ones allowed it to decay, simply because it was not their civilization, they did not care about it, and they no longer needed even to pretend to care.

This parallels the long history of Jewish anti-gentile massacres, celebrated in such festivals as Passover, Purim, and Hannukah. It also parallels the decay of gentile civilizations once Jews gain sufficient control to replace the natives with alien populations.

When the Innsmouthites discovered the narrator speaking to Zadok Allen, they decided he could not be allowed to leave. When the narrator showed up to catch the evening bus, he was told that it had broken down. (An obvious lie, since he saw it drive up.) He was told to check into the local hotel, the Gilman House (gill-man), and take the bus the next morning, after it had been repaired. Naturally, he was suspicious, so he locked, bolted, and barricaded the door and remained wide awake and fully clothed, ready for flight.

At 2:00 a.m., his electricity was cut off and someone tried to enter his room but found the door locked. The narrator climbed out a window and found the town on high alert. Vast numbers of Deep Ones were swimming in from Devil Reef, the roads out of town were blocked, and search parties roamed the streets. The narrator managed to slip out of town on the abandoned railroad tracks, but before his escape, he caught a glimpse of the Deep Ones in full repellent form.

The search parties were led by the robed and mitred priests of the Esoteric Order of Dagon and by the richest man in town, "Old Man" Barnabas Marsh, who was descended from Captain Obed Marsh on his father's side and the Deep Ones on his mother's. This parallels the leadership of diaspora Jewry by rabbis and businessmen. There is no Jewish warrior caste in the diaspora, because Jews are masters of manipulating others to fight and die for them.

In Innsmouth, the Deep Ones employed beings known as *shoggoths* to do their fighting. The shoggoths were a far more ancient race than the Deep Ones. According to Lovecraft's novella *At the Mountains of Madness*, they were created by the Old Ones, alien beings who settled the Earth in remotest prehistory and built a fantastic civilization. Although created as servants, the shoggoths ultimately rose up and destroyed their masters. The Deep Ones, however, seem to have tamed the shoggoths, and according to Zadok Allen, they had brought up large numbers of them and were housing them in boarded up buildings by the waterfront (p. 624).

Later, when the narrator is about to flee his hotel room, he hears, in addition to the furtive pattering of the Innsmouth folk, "the boards of the corridor ... groan with a ponderous load" (p. 632). I believe that the Innsmouthites had brought in a shoggoth for reinforcement. After fleeing the hotel, he sees "a small rowboat pulling in toward the abandoned wharves and laden with some bulky, tarpaulin-covered object" (p. 640). Another shoggoth, I suggest.

Lovecraft does not, however, merely tell of techniques of subversion. He also suggests means of liberation. Having escaped Innsmouth, the narrator traveled to Arkham and then on to Boston, where he told government officials what he had witnessed. Eventually, the Federal government was informed. In the winter of 1927–'28 they investigated the narrator's claims and, satisfied of their truth, launched a "vast series of raids and arrests" (p. 587) followed by the burning and dynamiting of a large number of buildings along the waterfront (the lairs of the shoggoths).

The press was fed the story that this was part of the war on liquor, but many were puzzled by the unusually large force of men making the raids, the secrecy in which they were conducted, the large numbers of arrests, and the facts that nobody was ever charged or tried, and none of the arrestees found their way to the nation's jails. There were rumors of "disease and concentration camps" and later of "dispersal in various naval and military prisons" (p. 587).

When liberal groups protested, their leaders were invited to visit certain camps and prisons, after which they fell silent. Nobody knew what to make of the rumor that a submarine had discharged torpedoes into the marine abyss at the foot of Devil Reef. Eventually, the raids were forgotten, and Innsmouth began to show signs of revived human habitation, bringing us to the narrator's present.

In short, Lovecraft believed it was both necessary and possible to secretly exterminate the Deep Ones through police and military action, destroying their habitations and confining the survivors in concentration camps and prisons. Today, of course, mention of concentration camps brings to mind Nazi Germany, but when Lovecraft wrote in 1931, Hitler had not yet come to power.

However, the concentration camp had already been invented by the British during the Second Anglo-Boer War of 1899–1902. Furthermore, concentration camps had been employed as tools of genocide in 1915 by the Turks against the Armenians, Assyrians, and Pontic Greeks. And by 1931, a vast network of labor camps had been established in Soviet Russia. Lovecraft was well-aware of these facts.

Zadok Allen also speaks of magical means of warding off the Deep Ones, who would occasionally boast that they had the power to wipe out all of humanity, except those who were protected by certain magical signs associated with the Old Ones (p. 615). When the Kanakys who mixed with the Deep Ones were exterminated by their neighbors, Captain Marsh found charms left behind by the invaders to ward off the Deep Ones. They were inscribed with the sign of the swastika (p. 617).

Counter-Currents, August 17, 2015

Philip K. Dick's *Do Androids Dream of Electric Sheep?*

Philip K. Dick's 1968 science fiction novel *Do Androids Dream of Electric Sheep?* is far less famous than Ridley Scott's 1982 movie *Blade Runner*, which is loosely based on the novel. A few of the novel's characters and dramatic situations, as well as bits of dialogue, found their way into *Blade Runner*, often shorn of the context in which they made sense. But the movie and novel dramatically diverge on the fundamental question of what makes human beings different from androids, and in terms of the "myths" that provide the deep structure of their stories.[1]

In *Blade Runner*, what separates androids from humans is their lack of memories, whereas in the novel it is their lack of empathy. In the novel, the underlying myth is the passion of the Christ, specifically his persecution at the hands of the Jews (both the Jews who called for his death and their present-day descendants, who continue to mock him and his followers). In *Blade Runner*, however, it is the rebellion of Satan against God—and this time, Satan wins by murdering God.

Do Androids Dream of Electric Sheep? is set in 1992 in the San Francisco Bay Area, with a side trip to Seattle. After World War Terminus, the earth's atmosphere is polluted by vast radioactive dust clouds. Many animal species are extinct, and the rest are extremely rare, so animals are highly valued, both for religious reasons and as status symbols, and there is a brisk market in electric animals. (Hence the title.)

---

[1] See my review of *Blade Runner* in Trevor Lynch, *Son of Trevor Lynch's White Nationalist Guide to the Movies*, ed. Greg Johnson (San Francisco: Counter-Currents, 2015).

To escape the dust, most human beings have emigrated to off-world colonies. (Mars is mentioned specifically.) As an incentive, emigrants are given androids as servants and slave laborers. (They are called "replicants" in the movie, but not in the book.) These androids are not machines, like electric sheep. They are artificially created living human beings. They are created as full-grown humans and live only four years. Aside from their short lifespans, androids differ from human beings by lacking empathy. In essence, they are sociopaths. Androids are banned from earth, and violators are hunted down and "retired" by bounty hunters. (The phrase "blade runner" does not appear in the book.)

The novel never makes clear why androids return to earth, which is inhabited only by genetically malformed "specials" and mentally-retarded "chickenheads," who are not allowed to emigrate, and a remnant of normal humans who refuse to emigrate and are willing to risk the dust and endure lifelessness and decay because of their attachment to the earth. Earth does make sense as a destination, however, given the androids' status as slaves in the off-world colonies and their short lifespans, which obviates concerns about long-term damage from the dust.

I wish to argue that *Do Androids Dream of Electric Sheep?* can be read as a systematic Christian and anti-Semitic allegory. Naturally, I do not argue that this brief but rich and suggestive novel can be reduced *entirely* to this dimension. But I argue that this is the mythic backbone of the narrative and indicates that Philip K. Dick had thought a good deal about Jews and the Jewish question.

Historical Christianity plays no role in the novel. The only religion mentioned is called Mercerism, which of course brings to mind "mercy." Mercerism apparently arose after WWT, as a reaction to the mass death of human beings and animals, which led the survivors to place a high value on empathy. Given its emphasis on empathy,

Mercerism is an experiential religion, facilitated by a device called the Empathy Box, which has a cathode ray tube with handles on each side. When one switches on the Empathy Box and grasps the handles, one's consciousness is merged with other Mercerists as they experience the passion of Wilbur Mercer, an old man who trudges to the top of a hill as unseen tormentors throw stones at him. At the Golgotha-like summit, the torments intensify. Mercer then dies and descends into the underworld, from which he rises like Jesus, Osiris, Dionysus, and Adonis—and, like the latter three, brings devastated nature back to life along with him.

According to Mercer's back story, he was found by his adoptive parents as an infant floating in a life raft (like Moses). As a young man, he had an unusual empathic connection with animals. He had the power to bring dead animals back to life (like Jesus, although Jesus did not deign to resurrect mere animals). The authorities, called the "adversaries" ("Satan" means "adversary") and "The Killers," arrested Mercer and bombarded his brain with radioactive cobalt to destroy his ability to resurrect the dead. This plunged Mercer into the world of the dead, but at a certain point, Mercer conquered death and brought nature back to life. His passion and resurrection are somehow recapitulated in the experience of the old man struggling to the top of the hill, dying, descending into the world of the dead, and ascending again. (The incoherence of the story may partly be a commentary on religion and partly a reflection of the fact that our account of Mercerism is recollected by a mentally subnormal "chickenhead.")

If Mercerism is about empathy towards other humans and creation as a whole, his adversaries, The Killers, are those that lack empathy and instead exploit animals and other human beings. If Mercerism is analogous to Christianity, The Killers are analogous to Jews. And, indeed, in the Old Testament, the Jews are commanded by God to exploit nature and other men.

The androids, because they lack empathy, are natural Killers. Thus bounty hunter Rick Deckard explicitly likens androids to The Killers: "For Rick Deckard, an escaped humanoid robot, which had killed its master, which had been equipped with an intelligence greater than that of many human beings, which had no regard for animals, which possessed no ability to feel empathic joy for another life form's success or grief at its defeat—that, for him, epitomized The Killers."[2]

Of course, although the androids epitomize The Killers, they are not the only ones who lack empathy. Earth has been devastated because human politicians and industrialists had less feeling for life than for political prestige and adding zeroes to their bank accounts. This is precisely why Mercerism puts a premium on empathy. A scene in which the androids cut off the legs of a spider just for the fun of it makes clear why they must be hunted down and killed. Mercer commands his followers *"You shall kill only the killers"* (ibid.). If only *human* Killers could be "retired" as well.

The android lack of empathy is the basis of the Voight-Kampff test, which can detect androids by measuring their weak responses to the sufferings of animals and other human beings. (The rationale for the Voight-Kampff test is completely absent from *Blade Runner*, in which humans and androids are differentiated in terms of memories, not empathy.)

The Killers and the androids are not, however, characterized merely by lack of empathy but also by excess of intelligence, which for the androids expresses itself in intellectual arrogance and condescension toward the

---

[2] Philip K. Dick, *Four Novels of the 1960s*, ed. Jonathan Lethem (New York: Library of America, 2007), p. 456.

chickenhead J. R. Isidore. Intellectuality combined with arrogance are, again, stereotypically Jewish traits. By contrast, Mercerism, because it is based on empathy rather than intellect, can embrace all feeling beings, even chickenheads.

The androids Deckard is hunting are manufactured by the Rosen Association in Seattle, Rosen being a stereotypically Jewish name (at least in America). (In *Blade Runner*, it is the Tyrell Corporation, Tyrell being an Anglo-Saxon name.) The aim of the Rosen Association is perfect crypsis: androids that cannot be distinguished from humans by any test, even though this agenda conflicts with the aims of the civil authorities to root out all android infiltrators. Deckard notes that "Androids . . . had . . . an innate desire to remain inconspicuous" (p. 529). Crypsis is, of course, an ancient Jewish art, necessary for the diaspora to blend in among their host communities. The Rosen Association obviously has higher loyalties than to the civil authorities, and Jews are notorious for protecting their own people, even criminals, from the civil authorities of their host societies.

The Rosen Association tasks an android named Rachel Rosen (a *very* Jewish name) to protect rogue androids by seducing bounty hunters. Apparently, sex with an android creates something of an empathic bond, at least from the human point of view, which inhibits them from killing androids. Rachel thus plays the role of Queen Esther, the Jewish woman who wedded Ahasuerus, a mythical king of Persia, and used their relationship to protect her people and destroy their persecutor Haman.

One of the most surreal episodes in the novel ensues when Rick Deckard interviews android soprano Luba Luft in her dressing room at San Francisco's War Memorial Opera House. (In the down-market *Blade Runner*, she is Zhora, the stripper with the snake.) Before Deckard can complete his interview and "retire" her, Luft turns the tables by calling the police.

Deckard is promptly arrested and discovers that San Francisco has another, parallel police department staffed primarily by humans but headed by an android who, of course, watches out for the interests of his fellow androids. Granted, an entire parallel police department is a rather implausible notion. A more plausible scenario would be the infiltration of the existing police department. But the episode strictly parallels techniques of Jewish subversion in the real world. For instance, the fact that US foreign policy is more responsive to Israeli interests than American interests is clearly the result of the over-representation of ethnically-conscious Jews and their allies among American policy- and opinion-makers. Jews seek positions of power and influence in the leading institutions of their host societies, subverting them into serving Jewish interests at the expense of the host population.

When Deckard frees himself from the fake police department and tracks down Luba Luft, he notices that, although she does not come with him willingly, "she did not actively resist; seemingly she had become resigned. Rick had seen that before in androids, in crucial situations. The artificial life force that animated them seemed to fail if pressed too far . . . at least in some of them. But not all" (p. 529). This brings to mind Holocaust stories of Jews allowing themselves to be passively herded *en masse* to their deaths without so much as a *kvetch*. (This seems unlikely, for based on my experience, Jews do not lack self-assertion.)

The final anti-Semitic dimension of *Do Androids Dream of Electric Sheep?* is its treatment of the media. Only two media outlets are mentioned, one private and the other owned by the government. (Hollywood is also defunct. Dick's ability to envision the future obviously failed him here.) The privately owned media broadcasts the same talk show, *Buster Friendly and His Friendly Friends*, on both radio and television 23 hours a day. How is this possible? Buster and his friends are androids, of course. But who owns Buster and his friends? The Killers, i.e., the Jews and their spiritual equivalents.

This can be inferred from the fact that Buster and his friends make a point of mocking Mercerism, just as the Jewish media mock Christianity (pp. 487–88). Killers and androids are hostile to Mercerism because their lack of empathy excludes them from the communal fusion that is the religion's central practice. Thus Isidore concluded that "[Buster] and Wilbur Mercer are in competition. . . . Buster Friendly and Mercerism are fighting for control of our psychic souls" (pp. 488, 489). It is a struggle between empathy and cold, sociopathic intellect.

Near the end of the novel, Buster Friendly goes beyond mockery by broadcasting an exposé showing that Mercerism is a fraud. The rock-strewn slope is a sound stage, the moonlit sky a painted backdrop, and Mercer himself is just an old drunk named Al Jarry hired to act the part of the suffering savior. Mercerism, we are told, is merely a mind control device manipulated by politicians to make the public more tractable—just the opiate of the masses.

The androids are delighted, of course, because if Mercerism is a fraud, then maybe so too is empathy, the one thing that allegedly separates androids from human beings. And empathy *can* be fake, because in the very first chapter of the novel, we learn of the existence of a device called the Penfield Mood Organ, which can induce any mood imaginable if you just input the correct code.

The exposé is true. But none of it matters, because the magic of Mercerism still works. J. R. Isidore has a vision of Mercer without the empathy box, and Mercer gives him the spider mutilated by the androids, miraculously restored to life. Mercer himself admits the truth of the exposé to Isidore, but still it does not matter. Then Mercer appears to Deckard and helps him kill the remaining androids. Near the end of the novel, Mercer appears to Deckard again and leads him to a toad, a species previously thought to be extinct, which deeply consoles Deckard. His wife Iran, however, discovers the toad is mechanical. The spider probably is as well. But even these fake animals do not undermine the healing magic of Mercerism.

I wish to suggest that Dick's point is that the historical dimension of Mercerism—and, by implication, of Christianity—does not matter. It can all be fake: the incarnation, the sacrifices, even the miracles can be fake. But the magic still works. This is, in short, a version of the Gnostic doctrine of "Docetism": the idea that the Christ is an entirely spiritual being and his outward manifestations, including the incarnation, are not metaphysically real.

This may be the sense of J. R. Isidore's perhaps crackbrained account of a widespread view of Mercer's nature: ". . . Mercer, he reflected, isn't a human being; he evidently is an entity from the stars, superimposed on our culture by a cosmic template. At least that's what I've heard people say . . ." (p. 484). A more likely account is that Mercer is a spiritual entity who takes on material forms imposed by our cultural template. Mercer can also employ technological fakery, such as Penfield Mood Organs, mechanical animals, and cheap cinematic tricks, to effect genuine spiritual transformations.

If this is the case, then *Do Androids Dream of Electric Sheep?* can be read as offering the template of a revived Gnostic Christianity that is immune to the Jewish culture of critique.

Counter-Currents, April 4, 2014

Afterword

When I decided to become an open white advocate, I simply dropped all contact with people I knew in academia. In case the enforcers of political correctness approached them, I wanted them to be able to say honestly that they had lost touch with me long ago. Frankly, I also wanted to spare myself the experience of being snubbed by them when my politics came up. I violated that policy twice by getting in touch with old contacts, and in both cases, I regretted it.

I should have extended that policy to making new contacts in academia as well. But when a commenter at *Counter-Currents* suggested I submit my *Androids* essay to a scholarly conference on Dick taking place at Cal State Fullerton in the spring of 2016, I submitted it on a whim, in unaltered form, thinking that if it were accepted, I would expand upon it considerably. For one thing, I needed to take into account existing Dick scholarship. I was pleasantly surprised when it was accepted for the program.

After the program was announced, however, my title piqued the interests of Jewish antisemitism monitors, who looked into me. Then they contacted the conference organizer, David Sandner, a professor at Cal State Fullerton, who immediately dropped me from the program when he was made aware of my views.

Sandner dropped me on the pretext that the essay had been previously published. I didn't think that was fair, since many conferences accept papers based simply on an abstract, and I viewed the published essay as merely the seed of the more academic paper I planned to present. But still, I felt bad for exposing Dr. Sandner to the PC terror.

I only found out about the behind-the-scenes machinations that led to my disinvitation much later from an article on the *Jewish Journal of Los Angeles* website.[3] And that's how my second academic career was nipped in the bud.

---

[3] "Philip K. Dick Conference Disinvites White Separatist," *Jewish Journal*, April 26, 2016.

MICHEL HOUELLEBECQ'S *SUBMISSION*

Michel Houellebecq
Submission
Trans. Lorin Stein
London: Heinemann, 2015

Michel Houellebecq is one of the finest novelists living today. His most recent novel, *Submission*, confirms my long-held suspicion that Houellebecq is a man of the Right, whether or not he admits it to us, or even to himself.

Houellebecq has long been one of the most savage critics of liberal decadence and cant. But *Submission* reveals that he is also a student of far-Right literature, showing a broad familiarity with demographics, eugenics, Traditionalism, European nationalism, distributism, biological race and sex differences, Identitarianism (which he calls "Indigenous Europeanism" in the book), and the critics of Islam.

Submission (a translation of "Islam") tells of a Muslim takeover in France in 2022. The National Front and a fictional Muslim Brotherhood party make it into the runoff in the French national election. On election day, they are neck and neck. Ballot boxes are stolen, invalidating the entire vote. Another vote is scheduled for the following Sunday, but in the meantime, the conservative and Socialist parties join the Muslims in a "Republican Front" to keep Marine Le Pen out of power.

Once installed, the Muslim Brotherhood institutes sweeping educational, economic, and foreign policy reforms designed to make Muslim hegemony permanent. Belgium is the next to fall, but all of Europe is doomed due to the political and economic integration of the Muslim world into the European Union.

Houellebecq's scenario is highly unlikely, at least in the time-frame he specifies. But lack of realism does not prevent science fiction from being an instructive mirror for modern society, and the same is true of *Submission*, which is less about Islam than about the weaknesses of modern France—and of its would-be defenders on the radical Right—that make them susceptible to a Muslim takeover.

Although millions will read this book, I believe that its chosen audience are the intellectuals and activists of the nationalist Right. Houellebecq wants us to succeed. He wants us to save Western civilization. But he does not think we are quite up to the task, so he offers some sage advice.

THE END OF DEMOCRACY

The first lesson of *Submission* concerns the political process. The Left and the center-Right are both committed to dissolving France into Europe and then into global "humanity." They are more opposed to French nationalism than to Islam, even though Islam represents a repudiation of their liberal and Republican values. They hate the National Front, and the nation it represents, more than they love themselves and their values. Therefore, out of suicidal spite, they would be willing to put France under a Muslim regime.

But wouldn't the Left and center-Right wake up eventually and resist as the Muslims began to implement their program? Houellebecq thinks not. The Left would be unable to protest because Islam is a sacred non-white, non-European "other," and the Right would be unable to protest because they are bourgeois cowards who follow the lead of the Left. The fact that both groups fear Muslim violence does not help either. (None of them fear

Right-wing violence, however.)

But if liberal democracy is a sordid, pusillanimous sham that is willing to deliver the nation and itself to destruction, then why is the National Front seemingly committed to democratic legitimacy? Putting a Muslim party in power is not politics as usual, in which power circulates between different branches of the same elite. It is the emergence of a new elite with a radical revolutionary agenda. Islam aims at irreversible change, hence it punishes apostasy with death. It is not just a flavor of liberal democracy that can be installed by a minor tantrum of the voters and then reversed on whim at the next election.

If this is how democracy ends, then *why is the Right unwilling to end democracy in order to save the nation?* Houellebecq sets up a scenario in which the only salvation of France would be a Right-wing revolution or military *coup*, followed by both massive ethnic cleansing and an *épuration* of the ruling classes, including "the *soixante-huitards*, those progressive mummified corpses—extinct in the wider world—who managed to hang on in the citadels of the media, still cursing the evils of the times and the *toxic atmosphere* of the country" (p. 126).

It goes without saying that the Muslims are willing to kill and die to get their way, but the Right, apparently, is not. In *Submission*, as in Jean Raspail's *The Camp of the Saints*, even the most martial and patriotic French are so rotted with humanitarian cant and cowardice that they allow their country to be destroyed rather than use force to preserve it. I refuse to believe that the French Right is quite that decadent and that Marine Le Pen or her successor would allow a great nation with a venerable tradition of revolutions, *coups*, and dictatorships to perish out of Anglo-cuckservative *good sportsmanship*.

Why are young Rightists not entering the French army and police forces? Why are they not opening private security firms? If none of this had occurred to the leaders of the National Front and the Identitarians, *it has now*. If so, perhaps Houellebecq will some day be remembered as the Rousseau of the next (and final) French Revolution.

POST-DEMOCRATIC LEGITIMACY

The next lesson of *Submission* concerns how to legitimate a post-democratic society. And make no mistake: even though the form of elections might be maintained, the Muslim Brotherhood would never allow itself to be voted out of power. Specifically, how would the Muslim Brotherhood neutralize its most committed enemies on the far Right, the traditionalist Catholics, the Identitarians, and the National Front? Simple: by instituting reforms that they wanted all along.

The Muslim Brotherhood is in no hurry to impose sharia law. The French may not fight for nation and freedom, but they will fight for alcohol and cigarettes. Christians and Jews will not be persecuted. The Muslims realize that the future belongs to the population that has more children and passes on their values to them. The native French population is shrinking. In a few generations, they will be virtually extinct, and those who remain will be powerless to resist sharia law. So all the Muslim Brotherhood has to do is wait.

In the meantime, they are content to reform the educational system, one of the bastions of the Left. Muslims are given the option of a completely Muslim education. Co-education is abolished. Female teachers are pensioned off. Schooling is mandatory until only the age of twelve. Vocational training and apprenticeships are encouraged. Higher education is privatized. The public universities are Islamized with huge influxes of petrodollars. Non-Muslim male faculty and all female faculty are given early retirements with full pensions.

In the economic realm, the Muslim Brotherhood eliminates unemployment by giving incentives to women to leave the workplace and return to family life. Small, family-owned businesses are encouraged through adopting Catholic distributist policies. Welfare spending is slashed dramatically, forcing people to work in good times and to depend on their families and religious communities in hard times.

In the social realm, the patriarchal family is reestablished as the norm. Women are encouraged to choose families over careers. Sexual modesty in dress, behavior, advertising, and popular culture are rapidly adopted. Oh, and Muslim men are allowed up to four wives.

Crime, which is a mostly Muslim problem anyway, plummets, perhaps because Muslims feel that France is now *their country*, and they no longer wish to trash it.

Now, dear reader, ask yourself: Wouldn't you wallow in *Schadenfreude* to see the Leftist academics, feminists, and welfare scroungers get theirs? Wouldn't you rejoice at such pro-family reforms? And that's the problem.

In the long run, under Muslim rule, France will disappear, and the only force that could prevent it is the far Right. But the far Right, like every other group, has a majority of short-sighted people and a minority of far-sighted ones. The far-sighted can only mobilize the short-sighted based on their present discontents. Drain the sources of discontent, and the far-Right constituency will grow complacent. And without followers, the leadership will be powerless.

The far Right is also a coalition of people with varying complaints. Only a minority are true racial nationalists who realize that to be French, one must be white. A black can be a French citizen, speak French, eat French food, and be a Roman Catholic. Thus citizenship, language, culture, and religion are not essential to being French. But whiteness is.

Many Rightists do not see this, however. They are broad-brush anti-modernists and reactionaries; traditionalists with a large or small "T"; anti-feminists, masculinists, and "Men Going their Own Way"; or devotees of dead or dying religions and deposed dynasties. Such vague and anachronistic yearnings will never be fully satisfied anyway. There will never be another king Clovis, who will re-Christianize France. So many of these people would be quite happy to live under a moderate Muslim regime that is traditional, patriarchal, hierarchical, and appeals to transcendent values.

After all, we have ample evidence of impotent Rightists being willing to accept vague approximations to their values and submerge their reservations, as long as the approximation is better organized and more active than the Right, which isn't hard. Thus in America, I have seen actual National Socialists converted into fervent enthusiasts for Ron Paul, Vladimir Putin, Alexander Dugin, Catholicism, Orthodox Christianity, Traditionalism—anything, really, as long as it appears to be a sizable and well-organized opposition to the existing establishment. You know very well what such weak reeds would do when confronted with an actual Muslim regime. After all, opposing Islam would be "anti-traditional."

There are many lessons for White Nationalists here. First, never let a Muslim regime come to power. Instead, prevent that—and gain power for ourselves—by any means necessary. Second, we must work relentlessly to focus our people on the paramount importance of race and not to fall for approximations and half-measures. Third, once we have power, we should not be in any hurry. All we need to do is hold onto power—which means postponing more radical reforms for a later date—and be content to set social processes in motion that will in the long-term lead to the sort of society we want. Focus on education and the family. Be kind to workers and small businessmen. Encourage the white population to grow and the non-white population to emigrate. Deliver prosperity, security, and peace to our constituents. And then wait.

THE JEWISH QUESTION

Now you may be wondering where the Jews fit into this. As Guillaume Durocher points out, Houellebecq hints at the importance of Jewish power, but in his narrative, Jews have no agency whatsoever.[1] They simply slouch off to Jerusalem when the Muslim Brotherhood comes to power. In France today, however, Jews are a formidable political force, and Muslims are far weaker than their numbers would predict. Indeed, Jews have played a dominant role in encouraging Muslim immigration and empowerment, and in stigmatizing French resistance. Perhaps Houellebecq thinks that Islam will turn out to be another *golem* that turns on its Jewish masters. Maybe he wishes to focus specifically on the susceptibility of the French to Muslim domination. Or perhaps he thinks that Jews can be persuaded to change sides, which strikes me as extremely naïve.[2]

SURRENDER & COLLABORATION

The next lesson of *Submission* concerns the psychology of surrender and collaboration. The main character of *Submission* is François, a 44-year-old professor of nineteenth-century French literature in Paris. (He is a specialist on Joris-Karl Huysmans.) François is an only child (of course), the offspring of two selfish baby-boomers

---

[1] Guillaume Durocher, "Houellebecq, Islam, & the Jews: A Review of Michel Houellebecq's *Soumission*," Counter-Currents, February 26, 2016.

[2] Greg Johnson, "Innocence of Muslims, Guilt of Jews, Interests of Whites," *Counter-Currents*, October 1, 2012.

(divorced, of course) of the type that Houellebecq so masterfully skewers in his other books. He has had no contact with his parents in years, and he learns of their deaths only after the fact.

François is obsessed with sex (of course, since this is a Houellebecq novel). He has never married (of course). Instead, he has a series of transient relationships with young female students, who always seem to be the ones who break it off (of course), perhaps to show how strong they are.

François' intellectual life is as empty as his personal one. The author of a brilliant dissertation, he has published one book, been promoted to full Professor, and now whiles away his time with petty academic politics.

Although a student of French literature, François knows very little about France. He seems utterly cut off from any sense of national identity. Left to his own devices, he eats nothing but Oriental, Middle Eastern, and Indian food, generally of the frozen or take-out varieties. (Let that sink in for a minute. How could any self-respecting Frenchman eat shawarma?) He lives in Paris' Chinatown. He envies his Jewish soon-to-be-ex-girlfriend's tribal identity, ruefully remarking that, "There is no Israel for me." (Yes, but who made it so?)

François is also a chain-smoker and a massive alcoholic, although these hardly distinguish him from other European men today.

Desperately unhappy, François tries to follow Huysmans' path into the Catholic Church, hoping it will provide a ready-made, all-encompassing meaning for his life. But it does not take. At one shrine, he has a quasi-mystical experience, but he interprets it as hypoglycemia. On another attempt, at a monastery, he flees after three days from the cold, discipline, deprivation, and forced sociability back to his solitude, cynicism, and cigarettes. Christianity demands sincere commitment, which François cannot give, and it offers very few creature comforts, which he cannot give up.

Naturally, François' utter self-absorption goes along with political passivity. He barely took notice of politics until his country was torn away from him, and then he did absolutely nothing to fight it. When he hears of the possibility of a civil war, he wonders only if the deluge can be postponed till after his death. The very idea of fighting or dying for France would never have crossed his mind. But men who care about nothing higher than comfort and security, no matter how clever and civilized they may be, are no match for men who are willing to kill or die for higher values, no matter how stupid and primitive they may be.

After the Muslim takeover, François is forced into early retirement at full pension. But then he is slowly reeled back in by Robert Rediger, a Belgian-born convert to Islam who is put in charge of the educational system. First, at Rediger's instigation, François is invited to edit an edition of Huysmans for the prestigious French publisher Pléiade. Then Rediger invites him to a reception, where they meet. At the reception, Redinger invites François to his home for a conversation, where Rediger reveals that he is recruiting distinguished scholars from the old system for the new Islamic University of Paris-Sorbonne. All François need do is convert to Islam, which he does.

Why does François convert to Islam rather than Catholicism? One reason is that Christianity is a feminine religion that inspires contempt, and Islam is a masculine religion that inspires admiration. But the main reason seems to be the fringe benefits. Christianity offered him swooning and self-denial. Islam offered him self-assertion and material advancement: a job at the Sorbonne, a huge salary, a house in a fashionable part of Paris, and most importantly, a cure for his sexual frustration and loneliness. Rediger offers him three wives, for starters: young, nubile, submissive Muslim girls to share his bed and bear his children.

Why does Houellebecq center his narrative on an academic? Because this novel is a thought experiment. Academia is the stronghold of the Left, which is still the strongest metapolitical force in our society, and if Islam can break its resistance, it can break anything else. Houellebecq realizes that academic males are pretty much all sexually frustrated wimps, dorks, and slobs: beta males oppressed by strong womyn in both their professional and personal lives. He believes they would welcome a regime that forces modesty in dress and advertisements, so they are not constantly tormented with sexual thoughts; a regime that restores male dominance in the workplace and bedroom; a regime that suppresses feminism and encourages female submission. Being married to four modern Western women sounds like hell on earth, but Islam might make polygamy quite workable. Houellebecq supports something I have long suspected: fundamentalist religions appeal to beta males as a way of controlling women. ("Jesus wants you to make me that sandwich, dear.")

Polygamy, of course, is not the white way. But Rightists need to take note. Today, feminism is probably the greatest source of misery for men, women, and especially children. White Nationalism is all about restoring the biological integrity of our race. That means not just creating homogeneously white living spaces for the reproduction and rearing of our kind, but also restoring traditional (and biological) sex roles: men as protectors and providers, women as mothers and nurturers. If we can promise to restore stable and loving families and homogeneous, high-trust communities, we can drain the swamps in which Leftists breed. After all, how many Leftists do you know who are lonely, dysfunctional, socially alienated products of broken families and communities?

Beware the Traditionalists

The most interesting character in *Submission* is Robert Rediger, first the Education Minister then the Foreign Minister of the new regime. He is a master of persuasion who knows that academics suffer above all from sexual frustration and unrequited vanity. He is a master of religious apologetic, meaning that he is an exceedingly clever liar. He claims that the Koran is a great poem of praise for creation, when it is closer to gangsta rap both as poetry and edification. He claims that polygamy is eugenic, which it might be if Muslims didn't marry blacks and their own first cousins.

Rediger is a large, masculine man, which makes him an unusual academic. But this comes as no surprise when we learn his history. As a young man in Belgium, Rediger was an ardent Right-wing nationalist. But he was never a racist or fascist, mind you. Just a broad-brush reactionary anti-modernist who wrote a dissertation on Nietzsche and René Guénon, anti-modernist thinkers with radically incompatible premises. This does not, however, prevent Rediger from shifting from one perspective to another whenever it suits him. Nietzsche destroyed Christianity for Rediger, and Guénon offered him a way into Islam, a religion he sees as more compatible with masculine and vitalist impulses.

The lesson here is obvious: if racial integrity is not paramount, then Traditionalism is a vector of Islamization. A demythologization of Traditionalism has long been on my agenda, and Houellebecq has convinced me to step up the timetable. Such an argument has two prongs.

First, as I argued in my review of Jan Assmann's *Moses the Egyptian*,[3] the Traditionalist thesis of the transcendent unity of religions is actually heretical according to

---

[3] Greg Johnson, "The Hatred Born on Sinai: Jan Assmann's Moses the Egyptian," *Counter-Currents*, June 28, 2014.

the Abrahamic faiths, Judaism, Christianity, and Islam, which reject all other religions as false.

Second, the Traditionalists are well aware of this problem. Thus their assertion that the Abrahamic faiths are compatible with Traditionalism is merely an attempt to trick their adherents into tolerating esoteric paganism. (Arguing this thesis would require a reading of Ibn Tufayl's *Hayy Ibn Yaqzan* and Guénon's *Initiation and Spiritual Realization* and *Perspectives on Initiation*.)

There is no Allah, and Muhammad was not his prophet. Therefore, whatever power Islam possesses is grounded in nature. If there is an overall lesson to *Submission*, it is that if our civilization falls out of harmony with nature and ceases to pass on its genes and values, it will be replaced by a civilization—no matter how backward and primitive—that is capable of doing so. And European man will disappear in a tide of fast-breeding, savage Sand People.

The Left and center-Right are deferential to Islam because they are decadent and devitalized. They sense its greater vitality, including its potential for violence. *These people want to be subjugated*, because no tyranny is worse than the fate of the atomized individual floating in the void of liberal, consumerist modernity. Liberal democracy and capitalism supply every human need, except to believe, belong, and obey. If our race is to be saved, then White Nationalists need to bring our societies back into harmony with nature. Whites must be forced to submit to *our own nature*, or we will end up submitting to aliens. And to do that, White Nationalists need to become an even more formidably vital—and intimidating—force than Islam. Clearly we've got work to do.

Counter-Currents, October 17, 2015

A Farewell to Reason:
Houellebecq's *Annihilation*

Michel Houellebecq
Annihilation
Trans. Shaun Whiteside
London: Picador, 2024

In terms of its emotional impact, *Annihilation* is Michel Houellebecq's finest novel. In his previous works, Houellebecq created and perfected a new genre of sorts: novels whose settings are worlds in decline, whose protagonists are utterly petty and impotent in the face of evil, and whose stories make me want to slit my wrists. *Annihilation* is different, though. It made me weep a bit for the protagonist before wanting to slit my wrists.

In *Annihilation*, Houellebecq has delivered a novel whose protagonist is slowly awakening from trivial egoism and emotional repression. Decency and even nobility are stirring within him. Sadly, it is too late to save his life, much less improve the world. In the end, *Annihilation* offers no solutions, just a few hints that the reader might build upon. But this is Houellebecq at his cheeriest.

It seems strange that Houellebecq's most hopeful novel is called *Annihilation*, but nihilism is the unifying theme of his work.

James Cameron's *Titanic* was silly, but one scene stayed with me: when the ship's engineer unfurls the blueprints and explains that, given the nature of the ship and the collision she had suffered, compartment after compartment will fill with water, and—no matter what they do from that point forward—the *Titanic* will founder.

Likewise, in novels like *The Elementary Particles*, Houellebecq unfurls the blueprints of modern society and the human soul, explaining that modern nihilism—

religious disenchantment, liberalism, individualism, consumerism, hedonism, feminism, sexual revolution, birth control, technology, capitalism, globalization—will lead inexorably to the degradation and eventual extinction of the human race. Beside Houellebecq stand thinkers like Vico, Nietzsche, Spengler, and Heidegger, all anatomists of decadence and men of the Right.

In *Annihilation*, however, it is hinted that even nihilism can be annihilated.

Annihilation is a combination of political intrigue and family drama. It is set in France in 2026 and 2027. Its protagonist is Paul Raison (Paul Reason). Raison is chief advisor to Finance Minister Bruno Juge (Bruno Judge), a mandarin who, under an unnamed center-Left President, has revived France's economy through protectionist measures.

Juge is targeted by cyberterrorists, who release a video showing him being guillotined. The video, of course, is fake. But its level of technical perfection is far beyond the industry standard, indicating that the people behind it have formidable skills and resources. The same terrorists also employ considerable resources and sophistication to destroy a Chinese container ship and a Danish sperm bank.

The French General Directorate of Internal Security (DGSI) first suspects Left-wing terrorists, perhaps ecoterrorists. When the sperm bank is destroyed, they suspect Catholic militants. But then the same group sinks a boat carrying 500 African migrants across the Mediterranean, machine-gunning the survivors. After that, they firebomb a secret laboratory in Ireland working on fusing human neurons with machines.

The DGSI then begins working up a new profile. Killing migrants sounds like white racists. So does destroying a Chinese cargo ship. Destroying a sperm bank and a laboratory fusing man and machine could be the work of Christian humanists, but it is also anti-technological and pro-nature. Maybe, then, they are dealing with ecoterrorists of the Right: eco-Nazis.

Ted Kaczynski and Savitri Devi are offered as examples. Both were deep ecologists. Both were also intellectually on the Right. Kaczynski didn't advertise that fact, but he spent a good deal of time criticizing Leftism from a vitalist point of view that is very much consistent with the far Right. Savitri Devi was famous for turning National Socialism into a religion. A fusion of their ideas is definitely possible.

Of course, it isn't a perfect fit. Kaczynski was a terrorist, but he wasn't racist and would not have used high-tech means. Savitri Devi, moreover, was pro-technology and would never have blown up Nordic sperm. Neither of them, moreover, would have a special animus for a French finance minister who was against free trade. It is also suggested that the terrorists fund their operation by shorting the stocks of the companies they attack. This is clever, but I can't imagine Savitri Devi or the Unabomber going in for such a thing. Finally, the terrorists use the Baphomet as a symbol. But Kaczynski had no truck with esotericism, and Savitri Devi had little interest in Western esotericism, especially anything smacking of Satanism.

Nevertheless, it is quite possible that both Kaczynski and Savitri Devi could have inspired such a movement, even though they would have disavowed aspects of its program and methods. As one intelligence analyst put it, "Today more than ever, power resides in intelligence and knowledge; and these ultra minority ideologies are the very ones likely to attract superior minds" (p. 391).

What is their goal? In the long-term, a better world. But in the short term, they may content themselves with simply "creating chaos, convinced that the resulting world would be a better one" (p. 391). This is not really nihilism. Indeed, the present system is nihilism. The terrorists, instead, are operating on the faith that after nihilism is annihilated, order and goodness will spontaneously reassert themselves.

Houellebecq's novels *Submission, Serotonin,* and now *Annihilation* show that the author has a more than casual acquaintance with the far Right: both canonical counter-Enlightenment thinkers like Maistre, Nietzsche, and Spengler, as well as less well-known figures like René Guénon, Savitri Devi,[1] and Ted Kaczynski (all of whom he mentions by name; he also mentions René Girard).

Houellebecq also refers to such Rightist movements and organizations as the identitarians, Civitas, and the National Front, now the National Rally. For instance, Paul's sister Cécile and her husband Hervé—"a monster of integrity, fidelity, and virtue" (p. 66)—are National Rally supporters, Tolkien fans, and believing Catholics. Hervé, moreover, had been a far-Right militant and still maintains contacts in that milieu, who come in handy in the story, when Paul needs someone to rescue his father from a hospital where he is being neglected. Houellebecq depicts Cécile and Hervé as decent and healthy people, in fact the only healthy couple in the whole book.

Interestingly enough, both Paul and Bruno himself have many views congruent with the National Rally. Paul, for example, hates jihadis and is disconcerted by the Great Replacement. He picks an Arab dentist only to avoid a Jewish one. He welcomes modern neopagan celebrations of masculinity. He regards the far Left with withering contempt.

Bruno, for his part, reads Spengler and Maistre, embraces nationalist economic measures, regards Leftists as fools, and has no illusions about migrants. The attack on the migrant boat created a shift in public opinion, which caused the National Rally to lose the second round of the

---

[1] I wonder if Houellebecq used my website the Savitri Devi Archive, www.savitridevi.org, in his research.)

French presidential election to a Zelensky-like center-Left candidate named Sarfati, a vulgar television comedian whose Sephardic Jewish surname means "French." Bruno is pleased that his party won. But he is also pleased that the terrorist attack will cause a downturn in immigration, which will make it easier to govern.

Both Paul and Bruno are distressed and puzzled by the collapse of marriage, family, and all forms of intimate relations. Sexlessness and loneliness are rising dramatically while birthrates are cratering.

> They had definitely screwed up, [Paul] said to himself, they had collectively screwed up somewhere. What was the point of installing 5G if you simply couldn't make contact with one another anymore, and perform the essential gestures, the ones that allow the human species to reproduce, the ones that also, sometimes, allow you to be happy? (p. 259)

Elsewhere, Paul muses that society depends on two institutions that are collapsing, yet there are no replacements in the offing nor any attempt to halt their decline:

> Family and marriage: those were the two residual poles around which the lives of the last Westerners were organized in the first half of the 21st century. . . . The liberal doxa persisted in ignoring the problem, in the naïve belief that the lure of material gain could be substituted for any other human motivation and could on its own supply the mental energy necessary for the maintenance of a complex social organization. This was quite plainly false, and it seemed obvious to Paul that the whole system was going to come crashing down, even if one could not at present predict the date or the manner in which this might occur—but the date could be close, and

the manner violent. So he found himself in that strange situation in which he was working steadily, and even with a certain devotion towards the maintenance of a social system which he knew was condemned beyond repair, and probably not in the very long term. (p. 383)

Bruno too is increasingly occupied with the question of decadence:

There was also something else, a dark and secret force which might be psychological, sociological or simply biological in nature, it was impossible to know what it was, but it was terribly important because everything else depended on it, both demographics and religious faith, and finally people's desire to stay alive, and the future of their civilizations. The concept of decadence might have been a difficult one to figure out, but it remained a powerful reality; and what was more, perhaps more importantly, politicians were incapable of influencing it. (p. 430)

Indeed, Paul actually wonders why Bruno does not support the National Rally, given his convictions. Paul could ask the same about himself. When he goes to cast a vote for Sarfati, he freezes then discards the ballot. He refuses to vote for the comedian, but he won't vote for the National Rally either.

In truth, Paul hankers after something even more radical. As he learns more about the terrorists, something terrible dawns on him: "the worst thing was that if the terrorists' goal was to annihilate the world as he knew it, to annihilate the modern world, he couldn't entirely blame them" (p. 223).

There is a great deal of inspired and cutting satire in

Annihilation. But it is directed entirely at the establishment, never at the Right.

I found the political thriller aspect of *Annihilation* quite fascinating, but it ran out of steam four-fifths of the way through the book. The terrorists taunted the authorities by releasing cryptic clues about their targets. The locations of the first four attacks corresponded to four points of a pentagram. The fifth point, therefore, gave away the location of their next attack: an island off Croatia where leading tech developers were planning to meet (very much the sort of people Ted K. would have liked to blow up).

Frankly, the whole pentagram device is more worthy of Dan Brown than Houellebecq. Real ecoterrorists would never have telegraphed their intentions like that, and they would have hit their most important target first, before rather than after the world knew of their existence.

In fact, the whole thing seemed so implausible that I suspected Houellebecq was setting us up for a plot twist in the last act. Maybe this was a ruse to throw the DGSI off track. Or maybe the "superior minds" attracted to this ideology were regime insiders, men with serious doubts like Paul or Bruno. But, sadly, Houellebecq just drops the whole thing, wasting a great deal of dramatic potential.

Instead, Houellebecq shifts his focus to the personal aspect of *Annihilation*, namely the life of Paul Raison. Paul and his wife Prudence are both children of French officials from the baby boom generation. Paul's father worked for the DGSI. Prudence's father was a judge. Both sets of parents were cold, selfish, and wrapped up in their work. Thus Paul and Prudence were relatively neglected and grew up like their parents, but even more emotionally damaged.

When the novel begins, Paul and Prudence are childless, even petless, and approaching fifty. They have been estranged for half their marriage, sleeping in separate bedrooms. They haven't had sex in six years. They barely talk to their parents, their siblings, or even one another. Given the character of Prudence's father, we are told, "there was nothing surprising about her turning out asexual and vegan" (p. 368). She was not named after a classical virtue. She was named after a Beatles song.

Both Paul and Prudence begin to thaw, however, when tragedy strikes their fathers. Paul's mother had been dead for ten years when his father, Édouard, had a massive stroke which left him almost completely paralyzed and in a hospital. Édouard's partner, Madeleine, and his highly religious daughter, Cécile, rally to his aid. They are joined by Paul's younger brother Aurélien, who is also emotionally repressed and in a loveless marriage with a journalist who is a memorably drawn monster.

Perhaps their father's brush with death shocked Paul and Aurélien into confronting the emptiness of their lives. But their courses of action were probably inspired by Madeleine and Cécile, both of whom are founts of selfless devotion sustained by a religious hope for the future.

Madeleine, in particular, had a very sad life. She had every reason to feel self-pity and self-absorption, yet she manifested only love, patience, and hard work. "Thinking of Madeleine's broken life," Paul "was filled by a wave of compassion so violent he had to turn away to keep from crying" (p. 154). This is a dramatic turn for such a cold fish.

As Paul learns more about his father's relationship with Madeleine, he realized that "his father plainly had access to levels of human experience that remained unknown to him" (p. 168)—things as mundane as having a joint checking account with his wife.

Similarly, Prudence's cold father revealed a depth of feeling she did not think possible when his wife was killed in an accident, after which he simply shrugged off his life and waited to join her.

For the first four-fifths of the novel, the story of Paul

and his family is every bit as fascinating as the political side. We watch with wonder as elementary particles like Paul, Prudence, and Aurélien begin to glom on to one another. They begin to open their souls and enjoy real human relationships once they enter the force-fields around their fathers, both of whom now transformed from selfish baby boomers into semi-catatonic Chakravartins. (They have not changed that much. Their self-absorption has simply been intensified to such a pitch that others must take care of them. Caring for others, however, is transformative.)

Of course, there are larger agglomerations of elementary particles than families, namely societies. Thus I thought and hoped that Houellebecq would bring the personal and political themes of the story together in the form of Paul's political awakening. But given the direction Paul was going, maybe Houellebecq thought that impolitic.

Unfortunately, Houellebecq's resolution of the personal side of the story is almost as anticlimactic as the political. Paul is promptly diagnosed with cancer of the mouth and jaw. The treatment is ghoulish. They propose to remove his jaw. But don't worry, they can cut some bone from his scapula and whittle it into a new jaw. Yes, they will also remove his tongue, but they can replace it with a chunk of meat from another part of his body. No, he won't be able to taste food or talk. But it's a small price for a Frenchman to pay for a 25% chance of survival over the next five years. Paul makes the right decision. He opts for less drastic treatments. Because eventually the cancer is going to kill him either way.

Throughout the whole ordeal, Paul and Prudence grow increasingly close. Their relationship is very moving, but Houellebecq's decision to dwell on their sex life is, frankly, grotesque. Love may have the power to make a 50-year-old woman in hot pants—or an emaciated man with mouth cancer—seem sexy. But Houellebecq's prose doesn't. In these spots, I feel that *Annihilation* is slipping back into the extreme pessimism and misanthropy of Houellebecq's earlier works.

Paul and Prudence find that love can sustain them in the face of death. But they realize that something more was needed for them to actually live: belief. Prudence wonders to Paul, "We weren't really made for living, were we?" Paul thinks she is right but rejoices that at least he was ending his journey through the world in her company.

"I don't think it was in our power to change things," Paul replies. In this context, "living" means the power "to change things." In the novel, other people have that power: Madeleine; Cécile, Hervé, and their identitarian friends. So do the eco-terrorists. But all of them are sustained by belief. Paul and Bruno were powerful men, but lacking conviction, at most they have the power to manage their decline.

"No, my darling," Prudence replies. "We would have needed wonderful lies" (p. 523). And there's the rub. In the novel, Paul has dabbled with Catholicism and Prudence with Wicca. But no matter how much they needed belief, their search was crippled by the premise that any sort of deep and life-changing conviction is untrue. Maybe they are "wonderful lies," but they are lies nonetheless.

In short, Paul and Prudence Reason are rationalists. But Paul is also convinced that rationalism is deadly:

> In fact, Paul reflected, that girl [his niece Anne-Lise] was leading her life with her remarkable degree of intelligence and rationality. He didn't think that in the long term rationality was compatible with happiness, in fact he was almost certain that in every case it led to complete despair; but Anne-Lise was still far from the age where life forces us to make a

choice and, if she was still capable of doing so, to bid farewell to reason. (p. 383)

Nietzsche's most interesting genealogy traces how reason becomes an idol to which people are willing to sacrifice their lives. Paul, it seems, is not capable of bidding farewell to reason, even though it makes him unhappy. In the context of the story, of course, there would be no point, because he is on the brink of death.

"Prudence," of course, is another word for reason, namely practical reason.[2] For thinkers like Kant and William James, practical reason can put theoretical reason in the service of life. But our Prudence is named after a Beatles' song, so maybe there's no redemption there.

Is the "message" of *Annihilation*—its "moral," even—that we should all "bid farewell to reason" while we still have a chance to live? Is simple belief—belief in *anything*—Houellebecq's prescription for overcoming the malaise of modernity?

I hope not, because it seems too simplistic. Even when you realize that individual freedom, sexual promiscuity, and capitalist plenty don't really make us happy, the main thing that keeps liberalism in place is *fear*: fear of the stupid, crazy, and evil things that religious believers do, things like the Thirty Years War.

We are not just suffering from too much reason but from too much freedom. We are in the grip of the idea that we have infinite real choices, so many choices, in fact, that we need reason to select amongst them, lest we be "arbitrary." But that's a false picture.

---

[2] For the philosophically inclined, I note that the names of Paul Reason, Prudence Reason, and Bruno Juge correspond to the topics of Kant's three critiques: the *Critique of Pure Reason*, the *Critique of Practical Reason*, and the *Critique of Judgment*. It may be a coincidence. It may be a joke on Houellebecq's part. But nothing in my interpretation depends on it.

Practically everything important about us is unchosen: our families, our genes, the nation and time we are born into, etc. Liberals call such traits "accidents" of birth, as if they are inessential to who we are, when actually they *define* who we are. Our most fundamental choice is to own up to this fact or to flee it.

In *Annihilation*, the most admirable characters, Cécile and Hervé, embrace and care for the world that is given to them, including their family, religion, and national identity. They do it with a sense of gratitude. The miserable characters—Paul, Prudence, Aurélien, and their selfish boomer parents—all had other plans.

In both personal and political terms, *Annihilation* presents identitarianism as the fundamental alternative to nihilism. That's an extraordinary message to receive from one of the world's most prominent novelists.

Counter-Currents, October 10, 2024

Frank Herbert, Our Prophet

It is just a coincidence that today's gathering falls on the birthday of Frank Herbert, the author of *Dune*, which is the best-selling and most influential science fiction book of all time.[1] Without *Dune*, there would be no *Star Wars*. Without *Dune*, there would be no *Warhammer 40K*. *Dune* combines tropes from science fiction and fantasy literature and explores deep issues in political philosophy and political theology. Thus I welcome an occasion to talk about Herbert, who is a true artist of the Right and a deep influence on my own political and metapolitical thinking. But be warned: Herbert had a wild imagination. So take a deep breath, relax, and let your imagination play along.

Mankind was born on Earth. But it would be a tragic failure if we were to die here. There is a deep truth to Oswald Spengler's characterization of Western man as "Faustian": ever desiring the infinite. And there is no better arena for the Faustian spirit than the exploration and colonization of the galaxy. Yet space exploration has been stalled for decades now. Mankind has not walked on the Moon in more than 50 years, much less reached for Mars and beyond.

Frank Herbert can offer an explanation for why mankind has spent the last half-century wallowing in the mud rather than reaching for the stars. Based on *Dune*, I think he would lay the blame at the feet of liberal democracy and capitalism, which are afflicted by increasingly

---

[1] This talk was delivered on Sunday, October 8th, 2023, at a Counter-Currents gathering in the Dallas-Fort Worth area. I want to thank everyone who helped organize the event and everyone who came out to attend. I love Texas and am frankly puzzled by its one-star rating.

short-term and mundane thinking. Indeed, the only reason we left the planet in the first place had less to do with Faustian striving than Cold War competition with the Soviet Union about which system—liberal democracy or Communism—would have dominion over the Earth.

Cold War competition was an enormous engine of technological development, especially in the West. It forced liberal democracies into some semblance of long-term strategic thinking. It also forced capitalists to treat workers more decently. The result was a golden age for Western workers, whose wages were buoyed by dramatic technological innovations, many of them lavishly subsidized by the state.

But the West's victory in the Cold War turned out to be our defeat, for two reasons. First, easing superpower competition removed one of the main spurs of technological development. Second, capitalism became global, and instead of increasing productivity through technological advancement, suddenly the craze became cost-cutting through offshoring production and importing cheap labor, the benefits of which accrued overwhelmingly to the oligarchs.

Increasing Leftist control of the culture led to the denigration of space exploration as white, male, and colonialist. Instead of taking humanity into the twenty-first century, the focus became uplifting blacks into the twentieth century—truly an infinite task, but hardly a heroic one.

So what kind of civilization could take us to the stars? Herbert gives the answer in *Dune*'s backstory. A galaxy-spanning civilization must cross vast distances, which takes an enormous amount of time. It must also spend enormous amounts of wealth today for the benefit of distant future generations. It would have to plan far into the future. Its form of government would have to be replicable on widely separated worlds between which travel and communication would be extremely slow and expensive.

It would, in short, require great decentralization.

Liberal democracies and capitalist enterprises are incapable of such great ventures. They only think of the next election or the next quarter. Wealth and power flow to those who better serve the whims of empowered morons in the present, not distant future generations. After all: What have future generations done for us?

Herbert believed that feudalism, not liberal democracy, is the social form necessary to take mankind to the stars. Thus in *Dune*, planets are ruled by hereditary dukes and barons who owe allegiance to a distant emperor. Feudalism is hierarchical but decentralized, befitting a world in which travel and communication are slow and expensive. Feudal institutions also supported long-term planning plus vast expenditures and multigenerational labors on matters that were far from mundane, such as building cathedrals and fighting for centuries against Islam.

Hereditary monarchies and aristocracies encourage long-term stewardship. Beyond that, initiatic spiritual institutions such as the Catholic Church and its various monastic and knightly orders—or, in the Muslim world, Sufi orders—provided the institutional continuity necessary to pursue plans unfolding over centuries.

In the *Dune* universe, three such spiritual orders emerged against the background of what Herbert called the "Butlerian Jihad": a holy war against artificial intelligence. In the pursuit of security and comfort, mankind had become enslaved by machines, and the only force that could overcome them was a religious revival. Only the sacred is powerful enough to trump the utilitarian and convenient. In the wake of the jihad, mankind had to do without artificial intelligence, which forced us to develop our own intrinsic powers.

The Bene Tleilax order created "mentats," human beings who had expanded their memories and analytical powers to the point that they could function as human computers. The Tleilaxu also practiced cloning and genetic engineering. Through something called "prana-bindu yoga" they developed "face dancers," human beings who could mimic the appearances and personalities of others. In the fifth *Dune* novel, *Heretics of Dune*, we learn that the Tleilaxu are Sufi Muslims, who take Islamic misogyny to revolting extremes.

The Spacing Guild focused on the development of prescient powers. To develop these powers, Guild Navigators used immense quantities of the most valuable substance in the universe: the highly addictive and consciousness-expanding drug known as "spice," found only on the planet Arrakis, known to its natives as Dune. The spice had mutated the Guild Navigators into strange fish-like creatures who could see the future, or different possible futures. They used this power to make faster-than-light travel possible by threading wormholes in space.

The third spiritual order is the Bene Gesserit sisterhood, inspired by the formidable nuns and crones the young Frank Herbert knew through his Irish Catholic grandmother. The name Bene Gesserit is supposed to call the Jesuits to mind and roughly means "Well Born," referring to the sisterhood's focus on eugenics. The Bene Gesserit also use the spice to prolong their lives and develop their mental powers. They use the "Water of Life," which is related to the spice, to access the ancestral memories of their female forebears. Through prana-bindu yoga, they have developed the ability to control the chemical processes and involuntary muscles of their own bodies by will alone. They have also developed other yogic superpowers, including a martial art known as the weirding way. By cultivating hyper-observation and abductive reasoning skills, the sisters have uncanny abilities to read people, which they call "Truthsense." Being women with seemingly supernatural powers, the Bene Gesserit were often disdained as "witches."

The sisterhood's principal occupation is eugenics. Their proximate goal is the breeding of a superman, who can transmute the poisonous Water of Life and access male ancestral memories as well as peer into the future. They call this Janus figure the "Kwisatz Haderach," which means the "shortener of the way." Their ultimate goal is murky, but it appears to be to ensure from any peril the survival and upward development of the human race. They are both the guardians and guiding intelligence of humanity.

Herbert was not so naïve to think that all of history can be foreseen and planned for. Some events are unforeseeable. But the Bene Gesserit planned for such contingencies by pursuing enormous power and also the supplest pragmatism, so they could quickly adapt to any surprise and counter every opposition.

The back story and world creation of *Dune* are not the only things of interest to political philosophy. The stories themselves also offer many lessons. The six *Dune* novels fall into three pairs.

The first two, *Dune* and *Dune Messiah*, tell the story of the rise and fall of Paul Atreides, the heir to a dukedom who becomes the Kwisatz Haderach, and while pursuing the world-shaking but still petty vendettas of his caste, unleashes a holy war that devastates the galaxy and makes him God Emperor over the ruins. Herbert clearly meant *Dune* and *Dune Messiah* to be cautionary tales about the dangers of charismatic leadership and mixing religious fervor with politics. These are sobering lessons our movement should take to heart.

The next two *Dune* books, *Children of Dune* and *God Emperor of Dune*, have become my favorites. They tell the story of Paul's son, Leto, who inherits his father's ancestral memories, prescient powers, and throne, but does not become an anti-hero whining about how oppressed he feels by his vast knowledge and power. Instead, Leto peers into the future, sees the extinction of humanity by one of its own inventions (AI again), and sets out to stop it. This task required 3,500 years of planning and execution. But instead of entrusting it to an initiatic order such as the Bene Gesserit, Leto found a way to fuse his mortal flesh with the larval sandworms of Arrakis, who produce the spice, becoming a monstrous colony organism that is virtually indestructible and immortal.

Humanity's greatest vulnerability is its political unity in Leto's imperium. Humanity can be ruled because it can be seen, and not just by the all-seeing God Emperor, but by all the forms of communication that make us available to and manipulable by great powers. Thus, Leto sets out to breed a strain of human beings who are invisible to the prescience granted by the spice. He also develops new technologies: a navigation machine that can replace spice-dependent Guild navigators and the no-globe, which is invisible to prescience and any other form of monitoring. The no-globe can be combined with a spaceship to create the no-ship, a stealth craft that can travel anywhere in the universe, unobserved and untraceable. Leto's goal was to engineer the scattering of the human race beyond the power of any single political order to surveille and control us, thus safeguarding us from any single point of failure. Leto's death—which Herbert models on the dismembered and resurrected nature gods such as Osiris and Dionysus—triggers the fall of his imperium and the scattering of humanity, thus securing our future. It is one of the most audacious and imaginative stories in all world literature.

The last two books, *Heretics of Dune* and *Chapterhouse: Dune*, are less successful as stories but filled with fascinating political ideas.

So in what sense is Frank Herbert a prophet of the New Right? In *Dune*, prescience is real, therefore so is prophecy. But Herbert was also very cynical about prophecies. The Bene Gesserit manufacture prophecies as a way to deprive people of their freedom. Many things are not inevitable. Many events are hatched and imposed upon us by scheming elites. Such plans can always be thwarted and opposed. But if you are convinced that certain events are inevitable, you will not oppose those who wish to impose them upon you. Indeed, you might help them. There's nothing inevitable about Herbert's vision of the future. But we can make him our prophet by making some of his memes real.

First, there is the Butlerian Jihad. We need to take the threat of artificial intelligence very seriously. AI is not a tool. AI is a new apex species which scientists are eager to create and give dominion over our planet. Then, they assure us, it will make our dreams come true. It is the daftest damned thing imaginable.

To get a sense of the folly of AI, imagine chickens laboring mightily to create a new being called "man" with enormous new powers and an immensely expanded consciousness that they literally cannot comprehend, all on the assumption that this new being will selflessly serve them (and I don't mean on a platter).

Ending up on a factory farm is the best-case scenario. It is more likely that AI would simply exterminate us as the only plausible threat to its survival, and it would decide this, wargame out all the possible counter-measures, and set its plans in motion 15 minutes after going online, while humans are still congratulating themselves on their brilliance.

We need to muster every possible resource to fight this madness. And the sacred always trumps the merely utilitarian. Thus we need a real Butlerian Jihad today, before AI goes online. Herbert was much too optimistic to think AI could be stopped after it gains power.

Second, we need to replace liberal democracy, with its short-term thinking and mundane values, with a social system that plans for the distant future, including mankind's biological and technological self-apotheosis and the exploration and colonization of other worlds. Everything that White Nationalists want politically is consistent with this ambition, as I argue in my essay "Technological Utopianism and Ethnic Nationalism."[2] No, I am not thrilled with all aspects of Herbert's imperium, some of which are clearly offered as dystopian. For instance, I strongly reject hereditary monarchy and aristocracy. But if we don't embrace Herbert's particular alternative to liberal democracy, we will still have to find *some* alternative.

Third, before we have the power to stop AI, halt the demographic and cultural decline of our race, returning it to the upward path, and plan for the distant future, we need to build institutions today that are capable of pursuing such ends. As I argue in my essay "Metapolitics and Occult Warfare,"[3] and as Herbert depicts in his *Dune* novels, the best vehicle for such world- and age-spanning ambitions is an initiatic spiritual order such as the Bene Gesserit—or the real Jesuits—or the Rosicrucians, Freemasons, and Sufis who inspired the Traditionalist writings of René Guénon and Julius Evola.

In my essay "Lessing's Ideal Conservative Freemasonry,"[4] I examine German Enlightenment thinker Gotthold Ephraim Lessing's critique of the Freemasonry of his day. Lessing was skeptical of globalism. He believed that the natural political unit was the nation-state. Yet he believed that nations, classes, and religions could fall into needless

---

[2] Greg Johnson, "Technological Utopianism and Ethnic Nationalism," in *Toward a New Nationalism*, second ed. (San Francisco: Counter-Currents, 2023).

[3] Greg Johnson, "Metapolitics and Occult Warfare," in *New Right vs. Old Right* (San Francisco: Counter-Currents, 2014).

[4] Greg Johnson, "Lessing's Ideal Conservative Freemasonry," in *In Defense of Prejudice* (San Francisco: Counter-Currents, 2017).

and destructive conflicts out of petty partisanship. To serve the good of the whole, it is therefore necessary to find men of all nations, classes, and religions who—although they may be passionately attached to their particular interests—are broad-minded and far-sighted enough to look beyond them to the common good. Finding such people, bringing them together, and empowering them to guide humanity was, for Lessing, the core of truth and goodness in Freemasonry.

Where do we find such people? Some of them may be seated next to you in this very room. How do we organize them? What do we do with them? As food for thought, I suggest you sample the highly addictive and consciousness-expanding writings of Frank Herbert.

Counter-Currents, October 10, 2023

ARCHEOFUTURIST FICTION:
FRANK HERBERT'S *DUNE*

If science fiction is quintessentially "progressive" and fantasy literature is "reactionary," then we need a third category for the six *Dune* books by Frank Herbert (1920–1986)—not to mention George Lucas' six *Star Wars* movies—which combine futuristic, sci-fi elements with the archaic values and magical universes of fantasy.

Fortunately, French New Right theorist Guillaume Faye has already coined the perfect term for this genre: *archeofuturism*, which for him is a kind of political philosophy and philosophy of history.[1] But it also captures a unique fictional genre which just so happens to be close to the hearts of many on the far Right, Old and New. (Faye himself ends his book *Archeofuturism* with a novella depicting the system he advocates.)

Dune, the first novel of Herbert's series, is the best-selling science fiction novel of all time. *Dune* is set more than 21,000 years in the future. Mankind has colonized the galaxy, creating highly advanced technologies—spaceships, glowglobes, ornithopters, lasguns, protective energy shields, etc. Entire planets, such as Ix and Richese, are devoted to advancing technological civilization.

Yet religion and mysticism are also very important in the *Dune* universe. Herbert shows how religion can be cynically used by the powerful as a tool of social control. But he also shows how sincere religious fanaticism can revolutionize societies. For instance, more than 10,000 years before the setting of the first novel, a religious war, the Butlerian Jihad, destroyed all artificial intelligences

---

[1] Guillaume Faye, "The Essence of Archaism," *Counter-Currents*, July 17, 2010.

and banned the creation of thinking machines. Herbert explores how ecumenical ideas—like the Traditionalist notion of the transcendent unity of religions—can be used to promote peace and tolerance, whereas exclusive forms of monotheism lead to intolerance and conflict. Finally, Herbert is very aware of the importance of religion and rituals of hierarchy and initiation in bonding together hierarchical societies, especially secret societies.

The ban on artificial intelligence forced human beings to develop their mental and physical capacities. Three groups have gone the furthest in this direction.

First, the Bene Tleilax have created mentats—human beings who can perform calculations, solve problems, and store data like computers. The Tleilaxu have also mastered genetic engineering, allowing them to grow human beings and other organic substances from isolated cells and manipulate their genetics. "Gholas" are cloned and genetically altered human beings. "Face dancers" are human beings which can take on the personality and appearances of other humans.

Second, the Spacing Guild has learned to replace computers for faster than light travel with the mental powers of its navigators, who are mutated humans with prescient awareness that allows them to pilot faster-than-light ships. (There is no talk of "folding space" and "traveling without moving" in Herbert's first four *Dune* novels. That comes from David Lynch's *Dune* script, and Herbert incorporated it into the final two *Dune* books.)

Third, the Bene Gesserit sisterhood is a quasi-religious order the goal of which is to guide the future evolution of mankind through eugenics. The sisterhood has also honed human physical and psychic abilities, endowing them with remarkable skills as fighters, mind-readers, negotiators, and all-round manipulators. The Reverend Mothers of the Bene Gesserit also share in the memories of all previous Reverend Mothers, which they pass along psychically to their successors.

Both the Guild and the Bene Gesserit are dependent upon a drug, the "spice melange," which has the power to extend life and expand consciousness. And, since the civilization of the galaxy depends on space travel, the spice is the most valuable substance in the universe. And it is found on only one planet: Arrakis, also known as Dune.

The Guildsmen use the spice to mutate their bodies and endow their minds with prescience. The Bene Gesserit use spice to expand consciousness. They employ a related substance, the water of life, to open their minds to the collective ancestral memories of the sisterhood.

Because, however, women are unable to expand their consciousness into certain regions through the water of life (for instance, male ancestral memories), but all men who take the water of life die, the Bene Gesserit are trying to breed a male who has the capacity to transmute the water of life and peer into pasts and futures invisible to the sisterhood. Their name for this individual is the Kwisatz Haderach, which means "shortener of the way."

Both the Bene Gesserit sisters and the Bene Tleilax gholas are capable of accessing memories that could not have been simply stored in a human brain. Thus Herbert's cosmos presupposes the reality of a kind of metaphysical dualism in which individual and collective consciousness (memory) can exist without a material substratum. Furthermore, both the Bene Tleilax and the Bene Gesserit practice "prana-bindu" yoga, which endows them with superpowers, meaning that their yoga is a Left-hand path that produces Tantric *siddhis* (superpowers).

The idea of a Spacing Guild, as well as hierarchical-initiatic orders like the Bene Tleilax and the Bene Gesserit, all of which are medieval institutions that wield what are, in effect, magical powers, place *Dune* firmly in the archaic and magical cosmos of fantasy literature.

There is swordplay as well as sorcery in the *Dune* universe: the galaxy is ruled by a Padishah Emperor, while many of the planets are ruled by dukes, counts, and barons who form a "Landsraad"—a college of noble houses. (Other planets, like Bene Tleilax, Ix, and Richese are equivalents of the medieval free cities.) It is an essentially feudal system.

Herbert, moreover, did not bemoan this system as repressive and unfair. Indeed, he regarded feudalism as a superior form of government, and one uniquely suited for mankind's expansion throughout the galaxy. Feudalism, unlike liberal democracy, is a highly decentralized system, which is suited to widely scattered planets and high transportation costs. Furthermore, feudalism, unlike liberal democracy, is capable of pursuing grand strategies over the vast spans of time necessary for space travel and colonization.

Because of the decentralization of power and costs of transportation, the different planets of the Empire develop very different cultures, some free, martial, and gallant (such as Caladan, ruled by the Atreides dukes—who trace their descent to the ancient house of Atreus), others despotic, sybaritic, and cruel (like Giedi Prime, ruled by the Harkonnen barons). But all planets have hierarchical, aristocratic forms of government. Herbert never has a kind word for liberalism or democracy.

In the *Dune* universe, martial and aristocratic values are dominant, and commercial values, although unavoidable and widespread, are regarded with aristocratic disdain. Great houses compete and ally with each other in accordance with iron codes of honor. Atomic weapons are outlawed. Laser and projectile weapons are seldom used because of the existence of energy shields, which can stop any projectile and destroy both attacker and target when they come in contact with a laser. Shields are, however, unable to protect from slow blades at close range, so high-tech shields are actually conducive to swashbuckling combat with swords and knives. Vendettas are governed by the iron code of *kanly* and can be settled through treachery or duels to the death.

Why do these novels have such a powerful appeal on the Right? The answer, of course, is that Frank Herbert was no liberal. No liberal praises feudalism over democracy, hierarchy over equality, and martial virtues over bourgeois ones—but Frank Herbert does. No liberal attaches great weight to heredity, speaks of racial memories, praises eugenics, and explains the Darwinian benefits of subjecting human populations to the ruthless culling of harsh environments—but Frank Herbert does.

Herbert believes in essential differences between men and women, which was uncontroversial when he began writing *Dune* more than 50 years ago, but today it is considered the height of reaction.

Herbert's novels are deeply and disquietingly anti-humanist and anti-individualist. He thinks in terms of the evolution of the human race over vast spans of time. He looks at history as a general on a battlefield, coolly sacrificing individual lives for the greater good. His novels are filled with well-drawn individuals, but that just makes it all the more poignant when they go willy nilly to their doom—or are resurrected as gholas to play another part in a larger drama.

Herbert traces the rise and fall of civilizations through great cycles, moving from vital and heroic barbarism to cynical, sclerotic, and decadent civilizations, which are then liquidated by fresh barbarians. (His view of historical cycles is closer to Giambattista Vico and Oswald Spengler, both of whom see vital barbarism as the first phase of history, as opposed to the Golden Age of the Traditionalists.)

For the sentimental and humanistic, the overall effect

can be bleak, depressing, and distasteful.

Aspects of *Dune* do, of course, appeal to the Left. When it first appeared in 1965, its ideas of mind-expanding drugs and sprinkling of Hindu terms found receptive ears in the counter-culture.

Dune can also be read as an anti-colonial allegory. Arrakis produces the most valuable commodity in the universe, but its people—particularly the Fremen of the desert—live in utter deprivation. Yet they dream of one day seizing control of Arrakis through guerrilla warfare and using its wealth to improve their lives.

This leads to a third theme in *Dune* which is popular with the Left, namely ecology, for the Fremen's dream was created by the Kynes family, both father and son, the Imperial Planetologists of Arrakis who set in motion plans to reclaim parts of Arrakis from the desert and create an earthly paradise.

None of these themes appeal to the Republican or libertarian Right. But the New Right can and does embrace deep ecology, Eastern spirituality, anti-colonialism/anti-capitalism, and even a bit of spice—together with Herbert's anti-egalitarian biopolitics—in a wider synthesis.

Counter-Currents, August 15, 2014

NOTES ON *DUNE MESSIAH*

Frank Herbert's *Dune Messiah* (1969) is the first of five sequels to his masterwork *Dune* (1965). It is the shortest of the sequels and I found it one of the least satisfying. The best sequels are *Children of Dune* (1976) and *God Emperor of Dune* (1981). The worst are *Heretics of Dune* (1984) and *Chapterhouse Dune* (1985).

John W. Campbell, editor of *Astounding Science Fiction* magazine, rejected *Dune Messiah* because he did not like the transformation of Paul Atreides, the hero of *Dune*, into a sulking anti-hero buffeted about by forces beyond his control. But this is not a problem for me, because Paul's reversal of fortune is a necessary outcome of the basic plot elements of *Dune*. In *Dune*, Paul Atreides' final step toward becoming a superman and conqueror is to acquire the power of prescience. He can see the future. But to see the future is to become imprisoned by it.

Paul saw that by using the wild Fremen of Arrakis to overthrow his family's enemy Emperor Shaddam IV, he would unleash a holy war that would engulf the universe, creating untold bloodshed and destruction. But he didn't stop it. Maybe he *couldn't* stop it.

Dune Messiah is set twelve years after the conclusion of *Dune*. The holy war is dying down, its chaos and fanaticism congealing into a massive, bureaucratic theocracy with Paul as God Emperor at the top. Paul is sickened as much by the peace as by the war. He longs for escape. He wants to free himself and humanity from tyranny, and not just political tyranny but the tyranny of prescience. He dreams of discrediting himself as a god and disappearing.

But Paul can't just step down without throwing the universe into even greater chaos. For one thing, he needs an heir to his throne, but for twelve years, his concubine

Chani has been unable to conceive. He refuses to have children with his wife, Irulan, Shaddam's daughter, for theirs was only a marriage of convenience, to secure his accession to the throne. But Paul is not too eager to have an heir, because he has foreseen that Chani will die in childbirth. It turns out that Irulan had been feeding Chani a contraceptive drug all along, but Paul forgives her, because he knows that it is prolonging Chani's life.

These are conflicts with enormous dramatic potential, and if Herbert had constructed his story around them alone, it would have been quite a good read. But instead, Herbert relegates these conflicts to the background, in favor of a Byzantine plot involving two conspiracies against Paul, one by Fremen and the other by offworlders: the Bene Gesserit, represented by Reverend Mother Mohiam; the Spacing Guild, represented by a navigator named Edric; and the Bene Tleilax, represented by Scytale, a "face dancer" who can take on anyone's appearance at will. But the aims of the plotters, and how they mesh together, are quite unclear.

The Bene Gesserit sisterhood's aims are clearest. They aren't seeking political power. They simply wish to continue their ancient breeding program by crossing Paul with Irulan or his sister Alia. They don't want Paul's heir to come from Chani, who is half-Fremen, a strain that the sisterhood regards as too "wild." But the purpose of their breeding program is to produce the Kwisatz Haderach, a Janus-faced superbeing who has access to his ancestral memories as well as the power to see into the future. But Paul is the Kwisatz Haderach, which means that their plans have already been fulfilled. Of course, the sisterhood wanted to control the Kwisatz Haderach, but none of their plotting could guarantee control over Paul or any of his offspring. So what's their point?

The Spacing Guild's motive is unclear. They do not seek political power. They simply seek a reliable supply of the spice that grants them the prescience necessary to navigate starships faster than the speed of light. But the spice comes from only one place in the universe: the deserts of Arrakis. So the Guild is dependent on whoever exercises political control over Arrakis.

The Bene Tleilax want Paul to renounce his godhood, discredit his priesthood and his sister Alia, and hand over his shares in the CHOAM conglomerate. One wonders if they have contemplated who would rule next or the chaos that would ensue if there were no clear successor.

The *Children of Dune* miniseries (2003) adapts both *Dune Messiah* and *Children of Dune*. It unifies the two novels by giving the plotters a common aim: returning Shaddam's House Corrino to the imperial throne. This improves the story considerably, because although it is a banal aim, at least it is an intelligible one.

As for the Fremen plot, it involves both Fremen who long for the old order and Fremen who have prospered under the new one. Their motives and aims are never made clear. Nor is it clear how independent their plot is of the offworlders' machinations. The offworlders snare Paul in their plot by revealing the Fremen plot. But it is not clear if they initiated the Fremen plot or simply discovered it and then used it as bait.

Beyond the murkiness of their motives, the actual mechanism of the offworlders' plot just doesn't make sense.

An essential premise of *Dune Messiah*'s plot is that one oracle can cloud the power of another oracle. The Bene Gesserit have introduced the Dune Tarot to Arrakis because even the presence of tarot readings can cloud Paul's vision. Guild navigators are far more prescient than tarot card readers, so the conspirators have included Edric the navigator simply to conceal them from Paul's prescience.

Paul knows that other oracles can interfere with his own prescience, but he nevertheless accepts Edric as the

Guild's ambassador on Arrakis. Why? Obviously, if one oracle really clouds another, he cannot anticipate the consequences. He knows there is a conspiracy against him, and he may wish to accelerate it, but it seems a mad gamble to do so while also diminishing his own powers.

Edric brings a gift for Paul: a "ghola," meaning a revenant. The Bene Tleilax have the power to grow tissue in so-called Axlotl tanks. They can take a cadaver, or even a few cells, and grow them into a living being. The ghola is the regrown flesh of Duncan Idaho, the Atreides swordmaster, who had died on Arrakis to save Paul and his mother Jessica from their enemies the Harkonnens. The Idaho ghola has no recollection of his previous life and has been trained by the Tleilaxu as a mentat (meaning a human computer) and a "zensunni" mystic.

When Paul asks the mentat-ghola what his purpose is, he says to destroy Paul. It is the most logical answer, but it is not the whole story. The Idaho ghola has been implanted with two compulsions. The first compulsion is to remember his identity as Duncan Idaho, which will be triggered when Paul tells him that Chani is dead: "When the moment comes, you will remember. He will say 'She is gone.' Duncan Idaho will awaken then"[1] The second compulsion is to kill Paul.

So the Tleilaxu do know how to bring back memories after all. Why do they wish to demonstrate this power to Paul in such a dramatic way? Because Chani is going to die in childbirth, and the Tleilaxu want him to know that they can completely restore her—for a price. But why offer Paul a deal and then kill him? A living Paul could honor their deal and protect them from his Fremen. A dead Paul could do neither. It makes no sense.

But the deeper problem is: How do the Tleilaxu *know*

---

[1] Frank Herbert, *The Great Dune Trilogy* (London: Gollancz, 1979), p. 538.

that Chani will die in childbirth? How do they know that Duncan Idaho will be present? How do they know what words Paul will use? Obviously, only prescience could make that possible. Paul knows, but he did not share that information with anyone, not even Chani. Thus the Tleilaxu must have had access to another oracle. *But the whole plot depends on the assumption that one oracle clouds another.* Thus if Edric hid the conspirators from Paul's prescience, Paul's prescience would have hidden Chani's end from any other oracle. Thus the Tleilaxu plot depends on knowledge that they cannot have according to the basic premises of the story.

None of this was explicitly clear, of course, when I read *Dune Messiah* for the first time. But I believe that my dissatisfaction was based on a subliminal sense that the central plot is incoherent. Now I understand why. Your experience, of course, may differ.

Counter-Currents, April 17, 2020

THE GOLDEN PATH:
FRANK HERBERT'S *CHILDREN OF DUNE* & *GOD EMPEROR OF DUNE*

Frank Herbert's *Dune* (1965) is one of the masterpieces of science fiction, far eclipsing its five sequels in readership and reputation. But I wish to argue that the third and fourth *Dune* books, *Children of Dune* (1976) and *God Emperor of Dune* (1981), are equally audacious works of the imagination.[1] Both volumes tend to be underrated, partly due to the long shadow of *Dune*, partly because the sheer scope of Herbert's vision boggles the mind, although this could have been avoided if he had been a more disciplined and focused storyteller.

Dune tells the story of Paul "Muad'Dib" Atreides, a man who becomes a superman, the "Kwisatz Haderach," who has access to the memories of all his ancestors and the prescient power to see things across great gulfs of space and time.

Paul is the son of Duke Leto Atreides, the ruler of Arrakis or Dune, a desert planet where the universe's most precious substance, the spice melange, is produced by immense and terrifying sandworms. The spice extends life and expands consciousness, allowing prescience and the sharing of memories. Memory sharing is practiced by the Bene Gesserit sisterhood, of which Paul's mother Jessica is a member. Prescience is developed by the navigators of the Spacing Guild, allowing them to pilot spaceships. But the powers of both orders only foreshadow those of the Kwisatz Haderach, perfected in Paul.

---

[1] Citations are to Frank Herbert, *Children of Dune*, in *The Great Dune Trilogy* (London: Gollancz, 1979) and *God Emperor of Dune* (New York: Ace, 1987).

When the Atreides are attacked by their archenemy, Baron Vladimir Harkonnen, in league with the galactic Emperor Shaddam IV, Duke Leto is killed. Paul and Jessica flee into the desert where they find shelter with the Fremen, the fierce and secretive people of the wastes who believe that an off-worlder born of a Bene Gesserit will come one day to lead them to freedom.

In his time with the Fremen, Paul's powers fully awaken. He builds an army, launches a guerilla war to lure the Baron and Emperor to Arrakis, then defeats them. The Baron is killed, the Emperor captured. Paul marries the Emperor's daughter Irulan, also a Bene Gesserit, and ascends the galactic throne.

Dune Messiah, the first sequel, is set twelve years later. Paul's rise was, naturally, contested. Countless planets rose in rebellion. Because the Fremen regarded Paul as a messiah and a God Emperor, the response was an immense holy war, which is now dying down. But Paul is also threatened by conspiracies hatched by his own Fremen, as well as the Bene Gesserit, the Spacing Guild, and the Bene Tleilax (a crypto-Muslim people who have mastered mnemonics, genetic manipulation, and other dark arts).

Paul is horrified by the crimes committed in his name and longs to discredit himself and the cult that has grown up around him. He is also oppressed by his prescience, for to truly know the future is to be bound to it. One loses even the illusion of freedom. As Paul's son Leto says, "to know the future absolutely is to be trapped into that future absolutely."[2]

Paul is blinded in an assassination attempt, but his prescient vision is unaffected. At the end of *Dune Messiah*, Paul's consort Chani dies giving birth to twins: a daughter, Ghanima, and a son, Leto II. Paul is astonished that his prescience failed to see Leto. This is odd, because one of

---

[2] *Children of Dune*, p. 638.

the central premises of *Dune Messiah* is that one prescient being blocks the vision of another.[3] Given that Ghanima and Leto both inherited their father's powers, he should not have been able to see either of them. But maybe their powers were not awakened in utero.

Suffice it to say that there is something special about Leto. Herbert believed that prescience was made possible by a strong version of determinism. We can see the future only if, in some way, it is already implicit in the present. Herbert then infers that if we are not visible to prescience, we must not be determined. That does not follow at all, since *not knowing* how one is determined is not the same thing as *being* undetermined. If this were true, then every prescient being is free insofar as he is invisible to other prescient beings but is also determined insofar as he can see his own future. But let us set this aside. Philosophers have never stopped arguing about the metaphysics of free will, and Herbert has a story to tell.

After naming his children and setting up a regency to care for them, Paul goes out into the desert to die, in accord with the Fremen custom of abandoning blind men to the desert, even though he can see perfectly well without his eyes. It is hard to understand the point of this gesture, since dying does not discredit Paul in the eyes of his worshippers. In fact, it completes his apotheosis.

Children of Dune begins nine years after *Dune Messiah*. Leto is still a child, but he has all of Paul's powers, both ancestral memories and prescience.

Leto peers into the future and sees that the human race will be exterminated by autonomous, self-replicating machines produced on the planet Ix.[4] To avoid this fate, Leto embarks upon the "Golden Path," which is the most

---

[3] See my "Notes on *Dune Messiah*," *Counter-Currents*, April 17, 2020.

[4] *God Emperor of Dune*, p. 348.

audacious project ever conceived by the human mind. Its goal is "the survival of humankind, nothing more nor less."[5] Leto called himself "the first truly long-range planner in human history."[6] The name "Golden Path" came to Leto in a vision: "I am on sand in bright yellow daylight, yet there is no sun. Then I realize that I am the sun. My light shines out as a Golden Path."[7] It is the way forward for humanity.

The Golden Path is far more than simply averting a technological apocalypse. It is nothing less than securing the freedom and the perpetuation of the human race.

Leto's first goal is to free humanity from the tyranny that prescience makes possible, even his own prescience. He wants to create a world "where humans may create their futures from instant to instant."[8] Setting aside the metaphysical questions of freedom and determinism, Leto's project can be understood as an attempt to liberate mankind from the plans of visionaries, including visionaries like himself. A huge part of his power, as well as the Guild's, is based on prescience. If they can see you, they can predict and control you. Thus anything that makes human beings less visible makes them more free.

The Golden Path is thus a plan to make planning impossible, a plan to increase the amount of opacity, contingency, and mystery in the world.[9] Thus, "Leto loved surprises, even nasty ones,"[10] because they were a sign that

---

[5] *God Emperor of Dune*, p. 13.

[6] *Children of Dune*, p. 861; cf. *God Emperor of Dune*, p. 166.

[7] *Children of Dune*, p. 627.

[8] *Children of Dune*, p. 826.

[9] This is the project of the Joker in Christopher Nolan's *The Dark Knight*, hence his name, which he connects explicitly with the wild card. See my review in *Trevor Lynch's White Nationalist Guide to the Movies*, ed. Greg Johnson (San Francisco: Counter-Currents, 2012).

[10] *God Emperor of Dune*, p. 22.

his plan was working. In *Children of Dune*, Leto says, "A universe of surprises is what I pray for."[11] Moneo, Leto's majordomo, thinks that Leto "believes in chance. I think that's his god."[12] At the end of *God Emperor of Dune*, Leto says, "Now, you see the mysterious caprices and you would ask me to dispel this? I wished only to increase it."[13] Leto's goal is a humanity that can say, "We are the fountain of surprises!"[14]

In Heideggerian terms, the Golden Path leads us from the *Gestell* to *Gelassenheit*, i.e., from a world in which everything is understood as transparent to human knowing and available for human manipulation—to a world in which contingency and mystery are signs that beings transcend our understanding and control; they have lives of their own. It is the path from subjection to freedom.

Leto's second goal is to scatter the human race to the far corners of the galaxy and beyond, so that at least some of humankind will always be out of reach of whatever malevolent forces may rise to threaten us. Leto says that because of prescience, there is no "frontier," meaning a place where men might escape. "There is now no place to go where others of us cannot follow and find you. . . . humankind is like a single-celled creature, bound together by a dangerous glue."[15] The "glue" is the dependency of space travel on the spice, which binds mankind back to the imperium. It is also prescience, which allows oracles to follow us. This is a form of vulnerability, for no matter how vast the imperium becomes, all of humanity's eggs are still in one basket. Changing that is Leto's greatest ambition.

Looking back on Leto's accomplishments, a historian

---

[11] *Children of Dune*, p. 639.
[12] *God Emperor of Dune*, p. 102.
[13] *God Emperor of Dune*, p. 420.
[14] *God Emperor of Dune*, p. 423.
[15] *God Emperor of Dune*, p. 273.

from the distant future writes, "How many universes have we populated? None can guess. No one person will ever know. . . . visionaries cannot *see* us nor predict our decisions. No death can find all humankind."[16]

It is never made clear how Leto prevented the Ixian apocalypse, but in *God Emperor of Dune* he says it would have happened by then if he had not prevented it.[17] It is clear, however, that Leto cultivated a close relationship with Ix throughout his long reign. Perhaps he guided their research and development away from self-replicating killing machines toward technologies that forward the Golden Path.

The first technology allows one to pilot starships without prescient Guild Navigators, who depend on the spice. The second technology, which Leto himself used, is the "no-sphere" or "no-globe," which is invisible to the outside universe, including prescience, whether of Leto, the Guild, or the Ixian navigation machines.[18] The two technologies can be combined into the no-ship: an undetectable stealth craft that can go anywhere in the universe. The no-ship makes it possible for humanity to scatter beyond the imperium, because it untethers humanity from Arrakis and the spice and is invisible to any would-be pursuers.

Another important element of the Golden Path is Leto's eugenics program. Leto seeks to breed human beings who are invisible to prescience and thus "free." Recall that Leto was invisible to his father's prescience while his sister Ghanima was visible. Leto proceeds on the assumption that this invisibility is a heritable trait. Herbert conceives this trait on the model of camouflage, the ability of

---

[16] *God Emperor of Dune*, p. 423.

[17] *God Emperor of Dune*, p. 345.

[18] One plot hole in *God Emperor* is that Leto discovers the Ixian no-globe near the end of his life (p. 375), but his journals were found preserved in one after his death (p. 1).

animals to become invisible to predators by blending into their background. It is a "new kind of mimesis . . . a new biological imitation."[19]

However, Leto's project of breeding more people with this trait focuses on the descendants of his sister Ghanima and her consort, Prince Farad'n Corrino. But why would Ghanima's children have a trait possessed by her brother but not by her? It only makes sense if *Leto was the father of his sister's children.*

To add to the confusion, Herbert maintains that the *official history* of Leto's reign records that he married his sister and fathered her children, but the *secret oral history* that Leto relates claims that the father of her children was Farad'n.[20] One wonders if this is just a case of Herbert literally losing the plot.

Leto's eugenics program is not gentle: "I have the cruelty of the husbandman, and this human universe is my farm."[21] His aim is "to be the greatest predator ever known" because "the predator improves the stock."[22] Leto's cruelty is magnified by the fact that his breeding program is practiced primarily *on his own family*. But the goal is to create a humanity that is immune to such manipulations and sufferings. At the beginning of *God Emperor of Dune*, Leto's plans have finally come to fruition in the character of Siona Atreides, his much-removed granddaughter or niece, who is invisible to Leto's prescience, and not because she is prescient herself.[23]

Leto understands the scattering on the analogy of launching an arrow with a bow. One pulls back the bowstring, creating tension. When one lets go, the tension

---

[19] *God Emperor of Dune*, p. 420.
[20] *God Emperor of Dune*, p. 289.
[21] *Children of Dune*, p. 868.
[22] *God Emperor of Dune*, pp. 16, 66.
[23] *God Emperor of Dune*, pp. 39, 350, 418, 420.

propels the arrow to its target. If humanity is the arrow, what is the tension that will propel it into the scattering? What is the release?

Leto creates tension by, in effect, bringing history to an end. He bottles up the creative, restless, and aggressive energies of the entire human race. In their place, he gives humanity peace and plenty, without change, for millennia. There is no politics, just the God Emperor's bureaucracy—and endless conspiracies to overthrow him. All social hierarchies have been eliminated—except, of course, the difference between the Emperor and everybody else.

Leto's empire is static, Pharaonic. Technological innovation is confined to Ix. The rest of the empire is low-tech. People have private property and trade among each other. Interest on money has been abolished.[24] All forms of travel, terrestrial and celestial, are minimized. Basically, people only travel for government business and essential trade, no tourism, no hitting the road just for fun. Space exploration—whether for science, adventure, commerce, or colonization—seems non-existent.

Many people would regard such a system as utopian. But mankind is not satisfied with peace and plenty. We are not satisfied with being satisfied. We are more than just producer-consumers. There is another part of the human soul, what Plato called "spiritedness" (*thumos*), that is the source of the love of adventure and freedom, as well as competition, conflict, and social hierarchy. *Thumos* is also connected with honor, manliness, and love of one's own.

The Atreides were known above all for their ability to cultivate *thumos*: they commanded loyalty from their armies and subjects by giving loyalty. They made a science of helping their friends and harming their enemies: "They could appear cynical and cruel to outsiders and enemies,

---

[24] *God Emperor of Dune*, p. 26.

but to their own people they were just, and they were loyal. Above all, the Atreides were loyal to their own."[25]

Surely then Leto gives *thumos* some outlet in his empire. After all, every government needs police and soldiers. But no, the enforcers of Leto's peace are *women*, the "Fish Speakers." I have no idea why Herbert chose that name. The Fish Speakers are, in essence, a sect of Leto's most fanatical worshippers who combine the functions of warriors, bureaucrats, and priestesses. Whereas male militaries are bound to their leaders by thumotic ties of loyalty and honor, the Fish Speakers are bound to Leto by religious devotion. They are fanatical Maenads. Which implies that Leto is Dionysus.

But although Leto makes a science of suppressing *thumos*, giving it no outlet in the real world, he also keeps the spirit of adventure and warfare alive in art and literature. According to Ghanima, the people "long for the Pharaonic Empire which Leto will give them. . . . They long for a rich peace with abundant harvests, plentiful trade . . ."[26] Leto remarks that, "The people of such a society sink down into their bellies. But when the time comes for the opposite, when they arise, they are great and beautiful."[27] They will inevitably arise because men are not just bellies. They also have chests, where *thumos* dwells.

When Farad'n asks Leto, "What will be the outcome of your peace?," Leto's reply is simple: "Its opposite."[28] "My peace is actually a forced tranquility," says Leto. "Humans have a long history of reacting against tranquility."[29] Leto is counting on that reaction. Leto keeps his populations

---

[25] *God Emperor of Dune*, p. 48. Cf. *Children of Dune*, pp. 731, 740.
[26] *Children of Dune*, p. 862.
[27] *Children of Dune*, p. 867.
[28] *Children of Dune*, p. 869.
[29] *God Emperor of Dune*, p. 92.

planet-bound, precisely because "It fills them with a longing for travel. It creates a *need* to make far voyages and see strange things. Eventually, travel comes to mean freedom."[30] "I have created a powerful spiritual tension throughout my empire," Leto says.[31] Obviously, one day there will be a huge explosion.

Leto expects that his death will be the trigger.

Leto never intended his empire to be the end of history. It is merely a pause and a gathering of forces for humanity's leap beyond itself into a radically new age of freedom, adventure, and exploration.

Like I said, the Golden Path is the most ambitious project ever conceived by the human mind. Such a project, however, would require unprecedented power exerted over an immense span of time: far more than a single human lifespan, even one prolonged by the use of the spice. One possible vehicle for such a plan is the initiatic order, like the Bene Gesserit, the Spacing Guild, or the Bene Tleilax, which can extend its founder's vision across millennia.

But Leto found a better way. In *Children of Dune*, Leto discovers something extraordinary about "sand trout," the tiny larvae that mature into the giant sandworms. He learns to fuse living sand trout to his skin. This gives him enormous strength and speed and makes him impervious to most weapons. The only thing that can kill him is water. Eventually, Leto morphs into a colony organism that looks like a worm-human hybrid, with a long sandworm body, a human face, and vestigial human limbs.

Leto's transformation first allows him to wrest control of the empire from his aunt Alia. Then it gives him the immense longevity necessary to carry out the Golden Path. At the opening of *God Emperor of Dune*, Leto has ruled the empire for 3,500 years, and his plans are finally

---

[30] *God Emperor of Dune*, p. 238.
[31] *God Emperor of Dune*, p. 385.

coming to fruition.

It is an agonizing transformation but a necessary one.[32] It is a lonely, loveless existence, but bent toward a noble end. Without it, humanity would perish. Leto has sacrificed his humanity to preserve the entire human race. But he has not given everything yet.

In *Children of Dune*, during the early stages of his metamorphosis, Leto fought against the ecological transformation of Dune set in motion by his father because he realized that it would ultimately destroy the sandworms. His aunt Alia (possessed by her grandfather, Baron Harkonnen) welcomed this outcome, since the Atreides controlled vast hoards of spice that would only rise in value if production stopped forever.

Once Leto was on the throne, he recognized the power such a monopoly would give him. The leadership of the entire galaxy was addicted to spice. Imagine their subservience if they knew the supply was now strictly limited and controlled by the Atreides. Thus Leto allows the ecological transformations to continue.

In *God Emperor of Dune*, the sandworms are long gone. They can return, however, but only when Leto dies. Then his skin will fragment into countless sand trout. Leto teaches his followers that each sand trout will contain a pearl-like droplet of his consciousness, in a dreamlike state. Eventually, the great worms will once again roam Arrakis, and the vessels of the divided god will bring forth the spice. Thus Leto's death will not just trigger the scattering of humanity. It is also his apotheosis. Leto will become another Osiris, another Dionysus, a god dismembered and scattered only to be resurrected as a bountiful harvest.

Leto's story is far more interesting than his father's. In

---

[32] Ghanima says, "One of us had to accept the agony, and he was always the stronger" (*Children of Dune*, p. 639).

Dune, Paul goes from man to superman. In *Dune Messiah* and *Children of Dune*, he becomes a self-pitying anti-hero ranting about the prison house of prescience and the evils of organized religion. He is entirely self-absorbed, from beginning to end. Were it not for his son, he would be a blight on the universe.

Leto is born a superman then transforms himself into a god who then dies and is reborn in order to save the human race. Rather than ranting about the chains of prescience, he breaks them—not just for himself, but for all mankind. He is a genuine hero, a savior, the real Dune messiah. As Ghanima says about Leto, "He gives more than anyone ever gave before. Our father walked into the desert to escape it."[33]

The full power of this story was, however, lost on me when I first read *Children of Dune* and *God Emperor of Dune*. *Children of Dune* struck me as more the end of Paul's story than the beginning of Leto's. As for *God Emperor of Dune*, I found it dreary and distasteful. The story arc as I have outlined it is concealed behind a great deal of clutter. Most of the characters, including Leto himself, are poorly realized. In six Dune volumes, Herbert never manages to communicate why Duncan Idaho is important enough to be resurrected repeatedly over five thousand years. Siona is not just baffling but also repulsive. There are immense swaths of repetitive talk, interspersed with action sequences that are often cursorily sketched. It really needed a rewrite.

God Emperor of Dune cannot be rewritten as a novel, of course, but it can be adapted for the screen. It has the makings of a magnificent movie. Indeed, what finally brought Leto's story home to me was the Sci Fi Channel's 2003 miniseries of *Children of Dune*, written by John Harrison, directed by Greg Yaitanes, and starring James McAvoy as

---

[33] *Children of Dune*, p. 861.

Leto. When I reread the novel, I was amazed at Harrison's masterful adaptation, which distills the essence of the story. I also was much impressed by Yaitanes' direction and James McAvoy's compelling portrayal. In fact, I wish they would team up again for *God Emperor of Dune*. If anyone can bring a 3,500-year-old tyrant worm to life, it is McAvoy. (For more on the miniseries, see my review.[34])

Dune Messiah and *God Emperor of Dune* are deeply reactionary and politically incorrect. The whole *Dune* saga is premised on the thesis that liberal democracy cannot give rise to a galactic civilization because of its inability to engage in long-term planning. Herbert's imperium is, instead, modeled on Medieval Europe, with a feudal nobility, guilds, and initiatic religious orders.[35]

We need an end to liberal democracy if we are to develop the science and technology necessary to deal with global ecological and sustainability crises, much less explore and colonize space.[36] We need someone to plan and act for the long-term interests of our race and the planet—to look out for the welfare of the world. A God Emperor who reigns 3,500 years is not (yet) possible. But we can build something like the Bene Gesserit, an initiatic order whose aim is to preserve, perpetuate, and improve the human race over the very long term.

As I have noted, Herbert believes in eugenics. He also believes in biological sex differences. Leto flatly declares that "There are behavioral differences between the

---

[34] Trevor Lynch, "The Sci Fi Channel's *Dune & Children of Dune*" in *Return of the Son of Trevor Lynch's CENSORED Guide to the Movies*, ed. Greg Johnson (San Francisco: Counter-Currents, 2019).

[35] *Children of Dune*, p. 664.

[36] See my "Technological Utopianism and Ethnic Nationalism," *Toward a New Nationalism* (San Francisco: Counter-Currents, 2019).

sexes."³⁷ When one character says, "The sexes can't be that different" the response (Herbert's response) is: "But they are."³⁸ For instance, it is precisely because women are less thumotic that Leto makes them his guardians of order. After 3,500 years of *thumos* being rapped on the knuckles by burly nuns, patriarchy is going to return with a roar.

Leto does not trust social reformers: "There has never been a truly selfless rebel, just hypocrites—conscious hypocrites or unconscious, it's all the same."³⁹ Leto finds that, "Liberal bigots are the ones that trouble me the most. . . . Scratch a liberal and find a closet aristocrat."⁴⁰

At one point, Leto casually observes that, "The new diversity on Arrakis could only bring violence."⁴¹

These books could never have found a mainstream publisher today.

Frank Herbert's saga of Leto II is one of the most ambitious, imaginative, and bizarre stories in all of world literature. Indeed, I can think of few stories that equal it. It is also deeply moving. The failures of Herbert's execution are not so serious that they cannot be repaired by readers with a vivid imagination, as well as a roadmap like this essay to guide them.

Counter-Currents, January 12, 2021

---

[37] *God Emperor of Dune*, p. 91.
[38] *God Emperor of Dune*, p. 206.
[39] *God Emperor of Dune*, p. 28.
[40] *God Emperor of Dune*, p. 185.
[41] *Children of Dune*, p. 732.

THE BENE GESSERIT BOOKS:
FRANK HERBERT'S *HERETICS OF DUNE* & *CHAPTERHOUSE DUNE*

Frank Herbert's six *Dune* novels fall into three pairs. *Dune* (1965) and *Dune Messiah* (1969) chart the rise and fall of Paul "Muad'Dib" Atreides, a man who becomes a superman and the God Emperor of the known universe. *Children of Dune* (1976) and *God Emperor of Dune* (1981) narrate the rise and fall of Paul's son, Leto II, a superman who transforms himself into a monster and rules for 3500 years. *Heretics of Dune* (1984)[1] and *Chapterhouse Dune* (1985)[2] are set 1500 years after *God Emperor* and focus on the Bene Gesserit sisterhood's struggle with their evil twin, a sisterhood that calls itself the Honored Matres.

The Bene Gesserit novels were great commercial successes for Herbert and his publishers, but artistically they are disappointing. The marvelous universe he built in the first four novels is still in place, but the stories take a long time to get going, with most of the action happening at the end—and often related in the sketchiest possible manner. The writing overall is prolix and self-indulgent. At one point in *Chapterhouse*, Herbert pauses to insert a soup recipe—and the story was not exactly flying along to begin with. The characterization is also weak, even for Herbert. But he was always more interested in recurring types than individuals anyway.

The great failure of the Bene Gesserit books, though, is thematic. The first two *Dune* novels are unified by the

---

[1] Citations are to the Ace paperback edition: Frank Herbert, *Heretics of Dune* (New York: Ace Books, 1987).

[2] Citations are to the Ace paperback edition: Frank Herbert, *Chapterhouse Dune* (New York: Ace Books, 1987).

grand, over-arching themes of religion and hero-worship, in both their positive and negative aspects. The second pair of novels focus on Leto II's Golden Path, which is arguably one of the strangest and most imaginative stories in all of literature. But in the Bene Gesserit books, there is no comparably grand thematic architecture to the conflict between the Bene Gesserit and the Honored Matres, giving the series a routine, "pulp" feel: there's plenty of conflict, but not conflict about anything that particularly matters.

This may in part be because the story is unfinished. Frank Herbert planned to write at least one more book to complete the story arc he launched in *Heretics*. But he died after publishing *Chapterhouse*. His son Brian Herbert, with Kevin J. Anderson, used the notes for "Dune 7" to write two massive novels, *Hunters of Dune* and *Sandworms of Dune*. But these novels read like vast pulps as well. One also wonders how much of these notes would have made it into a final draft, so I won't comment on them here.

Leto II's "Golden Path" was his attempt to save the human race from tyranny and technological apocalypse by freeing it from the Imperium. Humanity was fastened to the Imperium by two chains. First, there was the dependence of space travel on the hallucinogenic "spice," which is found only on one planet: Arrakis, also known as Dune. Second, humanity was fettered by the prescience created by the spice, including Leto's own prescience: the ability to abolish space and time and render everything present.

Leto severed these bonds in three ways. First, he worked with the Ixians to develop a navigation machine that could fold space without use of the spice. Second, he worked with Ix to create the no-globe, which made everything inside it invisible to all forms of knowledge, including prescience. The no-globe could be combined with the navigation device to create the no-ship, a stealth spacecraft that could travel anywhere in the universe unobserved, with no need to return to the Imperium.[3] Third, using his own family as breeding stock, Leto managed to create human beings who were invisible to all forms of prescience, even his own.[4]

But once Leto had assembled these elements, he still had to set them into motion. He wished to propel mankind outside his Imperium, to scatter us to every corner of the known universe, so no single gaze or power could encompass us, dragging us to our doom.

To create such an explosion of exploration and adventure, Leto locked the human race into a post-political, post-historical dystopia for 3500 years, suppressing human *thumos* and freedom while keeping alive a longing for them in literature and song. When the God Emperor died and his regime collapsed, both the chaos and the freedom that followed caused a great Scattering of humanity.

The Scattering was also a sorting: the most adventurous and aggressive fled the Imperium, leaving behind the most rooted and sedate. At the opening of *Heretics*, fifteen centuries have passed, allowing divergent evolution of the two populations—Imperium and Scattering. Conflict in the former Imperium is 2% of what it was before Leto's reign.[5]

It stands to reason that the peoples of the Scattering will be very different. Herbert envisioned them as warlike, competitive, and freedom-loving tribes. He believed that their ethos would generate immense diversity, wealth, and technological sophistication.

Eventually, some of those peoples would start finding their way back to the Imperium, driven by conflict or curiosity. Some of these wanderers might even look on the

---

[3] *Heretics*, p. 29.
[4] *Heretics*, p. 29.
[5] *Heretics*, p. 13.

Imperium as wolves look upon sheep.

After the death of the God Emperor, the Imperium lost central government. Sovereignty reverted to individual planets and planetary confederations. There is no talk of the Imperium's old nobility. The Spacing Guild is a diminished power because they have lost their monopoly on space travel. A religion has grown up around Leto II. It can mobilize the masses, but it is not a civilizational force because it lacks guiding intelligence and serves only to perpetuate priestly dynasties and prosecute impossibly petty feuds. (Herbert clearly despised clerics.)

The most powerful players in the old Imperium, ruling over uncounted planets, are two rival initiatic spiritual orders: the Bene Gesserit sisterhood and the Bene Tleilax brotherhood. Both orders are shadowy players in the first four *Dune* novels. In the last two, they take center stage, and here Herbert delivers handsomely.

Frank Herbert was fascinated by time-horizons. He believed that civilization required long-range planning, especially galactic civilization, due to the time needed to traverse interstellar space without faster-than-light travel. Liberal democracy, however, fosters short time-horizons and grants primacy to petty private interests. Therefore, it is incapable of the grand, long-range planning that will take us to the stars.

Instead, Herbert believed that interplanetary civilization would require the return of medieval institutions, such as feudalism (ideal for a decentralized realm spread over vast distances) as well as aristocratic dynasties, guilds, and initiatic spiritual orders, all of which are characterized by the ambition to persist through the ages, which requires collectivism, patience, and long-range thinking.

Herbert especially admired initiatic spiritual orders because they could survive for centuries, preserve and propagate their founding doctrines, and mobilize immense idealism and energy in service of their goals.

The Bene Gesserit sisterhood is modeled on Catholic religious orders. Herbert took inspiration from the formidable nuns and crones he was exposed to as a child through his mother's Irish Catholic family. The name is supposed to remind us of the Jesuits.

But the Bene Gesserit are hardly Catholic or celibate. They regard religion as merely a tool of statecraft. Their mission, moreover, is entirely this-worldly: the preservation and perfection of the human race. For thousands of years, they have presided over a eugenic program to improve the human stock. Many of the sisters breed prodigiously, but the Sisterhood allows no rival attachments, so most of their children are taken away and reared by others.

The Bene Gesserit have cultivated fine-grained conscious control of every voluntary and involuntary process of the body, which they use for enhanced health and extraordinary martial and marital skills alike. The Bene Gesserit also practice hyper-observation and abductive reasoning, which grant them "truthsense," an uncanny ability to read other people's emotions and intentions. Their powers are perceived as nothing short of magical, thus they are called "witches."

The sisterhood is especially interested in historical continuity. Thus they have developed a way to remember and pass on the memories of their female ancestors, but male lines remain obscure to them. Naturally, the Bene Gesserit also wish to develop the ability to see the future, as do the Guild navigators. Thus the principal goal of their eugenics program was to breed a male who could access both past and future. They called him the Kwisatz Haderach, meaning the "shortener of the way."

Five thousand years before *Heretics* begins, the Kwisatz Haderach was born Paul Atreides. But he escaped the sisterhood's control and shattered the whole Imperium, setting himself up as God Emperor among the ruins. His powers and his Imperium were inherited by his son, Leto II, known to the Bene Gesserit simply as the Tyrant, whose reign lasted 3500 years because he transformed himself into a monstrous hybrid of human being and sandworm.

Under Paul and the Tyrant, the Bene Gesserit were no longer in a position to pursue their own grand designs, but they demonstrated another feature of the best initiatic orders: the ability to roll with the punches, to adapt to and survive circumstances beyond their control.

After the death of the Tyrant, the Bene Gesserit became major political players in the ruins of the old Imperium. Their ultimate goal—the survival and perfection of humanity—remained unchanged but was tempered by their experience under Paul and his son. In particular, they were terrified at the prospect of another Kwisatz Haderach and ruthlessly killed anyone who showed such potential.

But they could not eliminate the Atreides bloodline altogether, because by that time, they were effectively all Atreides, specifically descendants of Siona Atreides, in whom the Tyrant's own eugenics program came to fruition with a genetic variant that made her and her descendants invisible to prescience and thus "free" beings—on the assumption that those who can be predicted are somehow determined. After fifteen centuries, practically the whole sisterhood is descended from Siona. Thus their fear of another Tyrant is specifically a fear of the malign potential lurking in their own blood.

But the sisterhood has arrived at a juncture in which a break with orthodoxy—a heresy—is required for the survival of their order and much of the human race, at least within the old Imperium.

In the first four novels, we learn that the Bene Tleilax brotherhood produce "twisted" mentats, namely human computers. (What makes them twisted, apparently, is that they have no ethical limitations.) The Tleilaxu have also mastered genetic engineering, using mysterious vessels known as "axlotl tanks," which can produce clones ("gholas"), hybrid organisms ("chairdogs," "sligs"), and even synthetic spice melange. But the most dangerous Tleilaxu invention is the "face dancer," sterile and servile humans of indeterminate sex who can take on the appearance of another human, male or female.

In *Heretics*, we learn that the Tleilaxu are a Sufi Muslim secret society. They are ruled by a small population of human "masters," who are tiny and physically repulsive men. They are served by a vast population of face dancer slaves. But the ultimate horror is the status of Tleilaxu women. They are the axlotl tanks: brain-dead female bodies hooked up to mechanical control mechanisms, mere incubators for mass-produced monstrosities. I can't think of a more brutal and contemptuous depiction of "oriental despotism" in all of literature.

In *Heretics*, the Tleilaxu have created a new kind of face dancer that they believe to be undetectable. Not only can it take on the appearance of another person, it can also absorb their memories and personalities, creating a perfect copy that just so happens to be a slave of the Tleilaxu. The Tleilaxu have been placing these face dancers in positions of power all over the old Imperium. Soon, they believe, they will be the masters of the universe. Only the Bene Gesserit stand in their way.

The Bene Gesserit and Bene Tleilax have existed for thousands of years, in a state of deep rivalry and distrust. They occasionally trade and cooperate. But they also plot against one another. Because both are secret societies, they naturally spy and counter-spy against one another, trying to learn the other's secrets while preserving their own.

One of the least plausible features of the *Dune* universe

is the ability of any organization to keep secrets for thousands of years, especially in a universe in which prescience in effect places us all in a panopticon. Herbert was horrified by the prospect of Artificial Intelligence. In fact, the distant back story of the *Dune* universe was the "Butlerian Jihad" that eliminated all thinking machines because they had enslaved humanity. Herbert died before the Internet and the "information age" came along, but he would have regarded them as sinister and dystopian.

The Bene Gesserit and Bene Tleilax are forced into an uneasy alliance by the appearance of the Honored Matres from the Scattering. By a combination of subversion and military force, they have taken control of a number of worlds in the old Imperium and now wish to challenge the major players: the Bene Gesserit and the Bene Tleilax.

The Honored Matres were apparently formed in the Scattering by renegade Bene Gesserits and members of the Fish Speakers, the Tyrants' female army and bureaucracy. They may have banded together simply for survival, but eventually they became a violent and predatory cult: paranoid, cruel, addicted to adrenaline and anger, and grasping after ever greater wealth and power. They are tactically shrewd but seem to have no long-term ambitions. They seek control over nature, not balance with it. Thus they are doomed to disaster.[6]

Despite their name, the Matres don't seem to be especially maternal. They control men by sexual bonding, hence they are called "whores," but they don't reproduce sexually. Instead, they recruit. All told, Herbert's characterization of the Honored Matres strikes me as hazy and muddled. They don't come off as feminists so much as wizened old biker chicks picking cat fights with one another.

One of the weaknesses of these novels is that most of

---

[6] *Chapterhouse*, p. 101.

the main characters are female. It is hard for men to write female characters, and it is hard, at least for me, to comprehend plots driven exclusively by female psychology. I felt I was drowning in an ocean of estrogen.

The most memorable character in these novels is Miles Teg, an Atreides descendant who looks remarkably like Duke Leto I. Teg was Supreme Bashar of the Bene Gesserit military forces until he entered retirement. He is nearly 300 years old, when he is approached by the Bene Gesserit leader Reverend Mother Taraza and asked to take charge of a project on Gammu, formerly known as Giedi Prime, the Harkonnen homeworld.

Teg is a military genius, but he's also a master at de-escalation and mediation who can win battles without firing a shot. He was steeped in the Atreides ethos of honor, loyalty, and service. His men are willing to die for him, and he is willing to lay down his life for the Bene Gesserit.

But Reverend Mother Taraza wants even more from him. She senses that Bene Gesserit orthodoxy and Atreides loyalty are not equal to the challenges ahead. She wants Teg to follow in the footsteps of his mother, a Bene Gesserit "heretic" who taught her son more of their secrets than authorized. This, of course, reminds us of another Bene Gesserit heretic who bore and educated an Atreides son: Jessica, the mother of Paul, the Kwisatz Haderach. Like Paul, Teg was also trained as a mentat.

Taraza senses that Teg has the capacity to become another Atreides superman, but instead of suppressing that, she wants him to commit the ultimate Bene Gesserit heresy and realize his potential. Which he proceeds to do. It is a rather inspiring story arc, and *Heretics* would have been a better book if some of the clutter were pared away to bring it into greater relief.

In *Heretics* and *Chapterhouse*, the Bene Gesserit are consistent mouthpieces for Herbert's anti-liberal sentiments:

Atreides ancestors rose up in rebellion at the word [liberal] . . . lashed out at the unconscious assumptions and unexamined prejudices behind the concept. "Only liberals really think. Only liberals are intellectual. Only liberals understand the needs of their fellows." How much viciousness lay concealed in that word![7]

Herbert believed that states can accomplish wonders. But he believed that their actions must harmonize with nature, and any attempt to flout nature would lead to disaster:

In my estimation, more human misery has been created by reformers than by any other force in human history. Show me someone who says "Something must be done!" and I will show you a head full of vicious intentions that have no other outlet. What we must strive for always is to find the natural flow and go with it.[8]

Herbert pours scorn on bureaucracies. Good government holds them in check, because nature holds it in check. Bad government, however, seeks the impossible, that is, the unnatural, which causes bureaucracies to grow in size and power until they destroy society:

A top-heavy bureaucracy the electorate cannot touch always expands to the system's limits of energy. Steal it from the aged, steal it from the retired, from anyone. Especially from those we once called the middle class because that's where most of the energy originates.[9]

---

[7] *Heretics*, p. 12.
[8] *Heretics*, p. 90.
[9] *Chapterhouse*, p. 155.

Bureaucracies also make societies brittle and incapable of dealing with change. "Bureaucracy destroys initiative"; bureaucracy hates innovation.[10] "Bureaucracy elevates conformity."[11] "Educational bureaucracies dull a child's questing sensitivity..."[12]

Herbert respects power, but he despises those who seek it. "Power attracts pathological personalities. It is not power that corrupts, but that it is magnetic to the corruptible."[13] "*Trust no government! Not even mine!... Power attracts the corruptible. Suspect all who seek it.*"[14]

Power is necessary. But if we cannot trust the people who want to wield it, then to whom should it be entrusted? Herbert's answer is that power should be thrust upon the deserving.[15] Aristocratic families, initiatic orders, guilds, and other institutions should breed and/or recruit those with leadership potential, train them, then promote the best candidates, who will also be the least willing. What, then, would motivate them? An ethos of duty, like the one cultivated by the Atreides.

Herbert values freedom, but he understands it in classical republican terms as self-government, not in liberal terms as individual license. Freedom isn't doing whatever you feel like. That is merely slavery to desire. Freedom, rather, is identical with duty, which is built upon disciplining desire: "Seek freedom and become captive of your desires. Seek discipline and find your liberty."[16]

The last two *Dune* novels incorporate some dark musings on banks and oligarchy. When Teg begins to size up the situation on Gammu, he realizes that it has become a

---

[10] *Heretics*, p. 213.
[11] *Chapterhouse*, p. 100.
[12] *Chapterhouse*, p. 115.
[13] *Chapterhouse*, p. 59.
[14] *Chapterhouse*, 138; cf. 154.
[15] *Chapterhouse*, p. 138.
[16] *Chapterhouse*, p. 344.

galactic Switzerland: a hiding place for immense wealth, including from the Scattering. But the banks also work as forward positions for a hostile elite that will soon arrive in full force: the Honored Matres.

Given Herbert's fascination with peoples who employ religion and crypsis to persist over eons, it is surprising that the Jews make their first appearance in the *Dune* saga only in *Chapterhouse*. I'm not quite sure Herbert meant it as a joke, but I laughed out loud to learn that they'll still be *kvetching* about Cossacks 30,000 years from now.

These wouldn't be Frank Herbert books without flashes of deep philosophy, such as Heideggerian ideas about science[17] and Sufi ideas about the magical universe[18] and active imagination.[19]

There are also brilliant feats of imagination, both grand (the depiction of the Tleilaxu worlds and society) and small (the Harkonnen no-globe on Gammu).

It is interesting to note that aspects of the *Dune* saga that contradicted David Lynch's *Dune* movie are in harmony with it here. For instance, in *Dune*, Giedi Prime is depicted quite differently than in Lynch's movie, where the Harkonnen keep appears as a vast black industrial block built above black, bubbling ooze in an industrial hellscape. In *Heretics*, the block appears with the name "Barony." Herbert also mentions that the ooze and other industrial blights have been cleaned up. Moreover, in the first four *Dune* novels, there is no talk of "folding space." But the idea appears in Lynch's script as well as in *Heretics*[20] and *Chapterhouse*.[21] Did Lynch influence Herbert, or did Herbert influence Lynch? *Heretics* was written at the

---

[17] *Heretics*, p. 148.
[18] *Heretics*, pp. 148–49, 176.
[19] *Heretics*, pp. 148–49; *Chapterhouse*, p. 242.
[20] *Heretics*, p. 69.
[21] *Chapterhouse*, p. 336.

same time as Lynch's *Dune* script, so the influence could go either way.

Herbert weaves such a tangled web that he sometimes loses his own plot. At one point, he mentions that the Tyrant had foreseen a woman who would ride worms.[22] But he could not have predicted the one who appears in *Heretics*, since she is a descendant of Siona and thus invisible to prescience. At several points, he mentions that the ghola of Duncan Idaho contains Atreides genes, which makes no sense if a ghola is a clone.[23] But the worst incoherence is on the thudding final pages of *Heretics*, when we are told that what has transpired was the grand design of Reverend Mother Taraza, when in fact it was brought about by Teg going off script and making entirely free and thus "heretical" decisions.

I see no point in ending with recommendations, since no force on earth could have stopped me from reading *Heretics of Dune*. But I will say it was worth re-reading. Despite its structural problems, it still offers genuine pleasures, and with a bit of streamlining, it could be magnificent on screen.

Nothing, moreover, could have stopped me from reading *Chapterhouse*. But nothing could force me to read it a second time. It is a pity that the *Dune* saga ended on a low note. But there's still some spice in these books. You've just got to sift through a lot of sand.

Counter-Currents, January 9, 2023

---

[22] *Heretics*, p. 4.
[23] *Heretics*, p. 467; *Chapterhouse*, p. 26.

WAITING FOR SAINT BENEDICT:
TITO PERDUE'S *MORNING CRAFTS*

Tito Perdue
Morning Crafts
London: Arktos, 2012

At the end of *After Virtue*, Alasdair MacIntyre concludes that modern civilization is bankrupt, and modern intellectual and political traditions are incapable of understanding and rectifying this decadence. He does not, however, counsel generalized pessimism, for once modernity expires of its own corruptions a new age will begin. Thus he recommends we follow the example of Late Antiquity, when

> men and women of good will turned aside from the task of shoring up the Roman imperium and ceased to identify the continuation of civility and moral community with the maintenance of that imperium. What they set themselves to achieve instead—often not recognizing fully what they were doing—was the construction of new forms of community within which the moral life could be sustained, so that morality and civility might survive the coming ages of barbarism and darkness. . . . What matters at this stage is the construction of local forms of community within which civility and intellectual and moral life can be sustained through the new dark ages which are already upon us. . . . This time, however, the barbarians are not waiting beyond the frontiers, they have already been governing us for quite some time. . . . We are waiting not for a Godot, but for another—doubtless very different—St. Benedict.[1]

---

[1] Alasdair MacIntyre, *After Virtue: A Study in Moral Theory*

I first read these words as a college undergraduate, and they made a deep impression on me. One sunny afternoon, I bought a copy of *After Virtue* at a used bookstore in Portland, Oregon, then embarked on a long train journey, during which I read it cover-to-cover. Much of MacIntyre's argument struck me then and now as relativistic and sophistical. But MacIntyre's final words resonated with my longstanding and steadily deepening conviction that Western civilization was heading toward a collapse. At that moment, I thought of creating a kind of monastery/college/commune in a remote location, in which Western civilization could be preserved not just in dead letters but in living minds, passed on from teacher to student until a new culture could emerge around them.

This idea has stayed with me, in one form or another, ever since, and it received its most adequate formulation when I discovered the Traditionalism of René Guénon and Julius Evola. In *The Crisis of the Modern World*, Guénon actually proposes the creation of a secret initiatic society to preserve the cultural treasures of the West through the crash of the current Dark Age and into the beginning of the next civilizational cycle.

One reason I found Tito Perdue's novel *Morning Crafts* so appealing is that it is set against the backdrop of such an intellectual ark, created to shelter the treasures of the West through the storms and deluge to come.

Tito Perdue was born in 1938 in Chile to American parents with deep Southern roots. His family moved back to the United States at the outbreak of the Second World War, settling in Alabama. He took degrees in English literature, European history, and library science. He worked in the Midwest and Northeast as a bookkeeper, a library administrator, and an insurance underwriter. In 1982, he took an early retirement and returned to the South to

---

(Notre Dame: Notre Dame University Press, 1981), p. 263.

write full-time, which he has done ever since. He has authored more than a dozen novels, seven of which have been published, *Morning Crafts* being the most recent.

Perdue's first novel, *Lee*, was published in 1991, to widely positive reviews.[2] His next two novels, *The New Austerities* and *Opportunities in Alabama Agriculture*, appeared in 1994.[3] The strong elitism and misanthropy of Perdue's novels, however, made his work increasingly hard to place in politically-correct mainstream publishing circles. Thus his next novel, *The Sweet-Scented Manuscript* appeared only in 2004,[4] followed by *Fields of Asphodel* in 2007.[5]

Since then, Perdue's books have appeared from New Right publishers: *The Node*[6] came out in 2011 from Nine-Banded Books; *Morning Crafts* came out in 2012 from Arktos; and Washington Summit Publishers will publish *Reuben* in 2013.[7]

Tito Perdue is America's finest living novelist. His genre is Southern Gothic, and his style is magical realist. His main themes are the nature of the good life and the decline of Western civilization. With the exception of *The*

---

[2] Tito Perdue, *Lee* (New York: The Overlook Press, 1991).

[3] Tito Perdue, *The New Austerities*, first edition (Atlanta: Peachtree Publishers, 1994); second edition (Brent, Alabama: The Standard American Publishing Company, 2023); *Opportunities in Alabama Agriculture*, first edition (Dallas: Baskerville, 1994); second edition (Brent, Alabama: The Standard American Publishing Company, 2023).

[4] Tito Perdue, *The Sweet-Scented Manuscript* (Dallas: Baskerville, 2004).

[5] Tito Perdue, *Fields of Asphodel*, first edition (New York: The Overlook Press, 2007); second edition (Brent, Alabama: The Standard American Publishing Company, 2023).

[6] Tito Perdue, *The Node* (Charleston, West Virginia: Nine-Banded Books, 2011).

[7] Tito Perdue, *Reuben*, first edition (Whitefish, Montana: Washington Summit Publishers, 2014); second edition (Brent, Alabama: The Standard American Publishing Company, 2022).

Node, all of his published novels (and most of the unpublished ones) relate episodes in the life of Leland Pefley, beginning two generations back with his grandfather and extending into the afterlife.

Lee Pefley is something of an *alter ego* of Perdue himself: like Perdue, he is born circa 1938; like Perdue, he marries a woman named Judy; like Perdue, he seems to be a lover of nature, of Western civilization, and of a simple but materially comfortable form of life; like Perdue, he becomes an increasingly angry and alienated as the civilization he loves falls apart around him, being replaced by urban sprawl, junk culture, and tasteless, degraded material opulence.

Morning Crafts is the best place to begin the saga of Lee Pefley. Young Lee is introduced at the end of *Opportunities in Alabama Agriculture*, but the book is primarily the story of his grandfather. *Morning Crafts* is the earliest installment of Lee's story published so far, although there is an as yet unpublished prequel about Lee, aged 11, called *The Smut Book*.[8]

The novel is set at the beginning of the 1950s. Young Lee Pefley, aged 13, is fishing near his father's Tennessee farm when a well-dressed stranger from the city beguiles him into his car and abducts him. The kidnapper drops Lee off in a remote location in rural Alabama, with a number of other abducted boys. The boys, of course, fear that they are to be molested or killed.

But their captors—Goldman, Arnsdorf, Spivey, and others—have something far more outlandish in mind: an experiment in education. Using shady sources of funding, they have assembled a group of kidnapped boys and a vast library of stolen books on a remote farm to preserve the

---

[8] Tito Perdue, *The Smut Book*, first edition (San Francisco: Counter-Currents, 2018); second edition (Brent, Alabama: The Standard American Publishing Company, 2020).

Western cultural tradition by passing it on to a new generation. Lee quickly determines that he can leave any time, but he decides to stay, because he discovers that he enjoys the life of the mind. His teachers, especially their leader, Goldman, not only impart languages, history, art, and science. They also teach a radically elitist and hierarchical critique of modernity. The core of the curriculum seems classical and pagan. But as far as their neighbors know, they are running a Bible Academy. This kind of dissembling, however, is also part of the curriculum. The educated man must always seek to blend in with the *demos*, lest they persecute him.

It all sounds vaguely Traditionalist. But it has its sinister aspects. Aside from the fact that the students were kidnapped, the books were stolen, and the whole operation was carried on under piously fraudulent pretenses, students are divided into Alphas, Betas, and Gammas. Gammas are basically treated as slave labor for the farm. One boy actually dies from overwork. They are kept drugged. Others are simply sent away, which takes on increasingly sinister connotations. At the end, it is strongly implied that they are to be killed. But this does not seem to bother Lee and the other Alpha boys, who are entirely absorbed not just with learning but with competing with one another, their insecurities and jealousies masterfully manipulated by their teachers.

I think that Perdue includes these unsettling elements to communicate that the aims of the teachers are so important that all more mundane moral considerations fall by the wayside. To save our civilization, we may indeed have to resort to extreme measures.

To my ears, the name Goldman has sinister connotations as well. I do not know why Perdue chose it, but it brings to mind three Jews who were associated with liberal education in the twenieth century: Mortimer Adler, Leo Strauss, and Jacob Klein. Klein was for many years the dean of St. John's College in Annapolis, where he presided over a "Great Books" program that joins together the best possible curriculum and the worst possible pedagogy: Mortimer Adler married, as it were, to Maria Montessori. Klein was a schoolmate and life-long friend of Leo Strauss. Strauss taught at St. John's at the end of his career, and many of his students found work there. Thus St. John's (both in Annapolis and Santa Fe) has a cultish atmosphere that is generically Jewish, with a dominant Straussian, neo-conservative strand. The nameless rustic Alabama academy comes off as a pocket parody of St. John's. When the locals and the police begin to get suspicious, Goldman and company simply torch the place and decamp to Mexico.

Morning Crafts is a classic *Bildungsroman*, a story of the awakening of the mind. One of the most effective scenes in the book is when Lee, having grown haughty with his knowledge, visits a remote Alabama cabin, much like the place in which he grew up. It is inhabited by a young man and his mother or grandmother. They offer him their hospitality, and Lee enjoys their simple food. He appreciates the beauty of their hand-made quilts and birdhouses, their ability to combine natural simplicity and material comfort. But the man has no way to appreciate Lee. His world consists of smoke, drink, food, hunting, and whores. As he drinks himself into a stupor, he keeps insisting that Lee has been "ruint" by his education. But this is simply not true: the educated man, especially a man of refined taste, can appreciate the simple life and even live it. Lee feels great tenderness for these collard-eaters, because he is one of them—or was. Back at the Academy, they also live off the land. They live simply, but they live well. Men of the mind can appreciate unintellectual things, even if they are beneath them. But unintellectual men cannot return the favor: they are blind to the things above them and incapable of loving them. This is why the wise must rule. But only if the wise who have a cultural and organic connection to the rest of the society, which brings us back to the Goldman problem.

My general preference is for tightly plotted novels. Perdue's work, however, is more episodic and chronicle-like, which makes sense, since he is telling the story of a life spread over a number of books. *Morning Crafts* is a succession of short chapters, vignettes separated from one another by indeterminate spans of time, leaving it to the reader to put it all together. But it nevertheless works because of Perdue's fascinatingly drawn characters and entrancingly beautiful writing. I have not taken such sheer delight in language since the last time I read Camille Paglia's *Sexual Personae* or Gabriel García Márquez's *One Hundred Years of Solitude*—and that is saying a lot, since it is my favorite novel of all time. I would have stopped every ten minutes and read something aloud, if I had someone to read it to.

Jonathan Bowden once said that the overwhelming decadence of our culture does not mean that the creativity of our race has disappeared. It has simply been marginalized and disprivileged. Thus there must be great white novelists, painters, poets, composers, and other creators out there. We simply have to find them, publish them, and promote them. We have to create new cultural spaces where the greatness of our people can flourish.

Tito Perdue is proof of this. Chased from the mainstream, he continued to labor in solitude until the New Right finally caught up with him. He has now found a community of writers, publishers, and readers who love his work and wish to share it with the world. You, dear reader, need to join them. I cannot recommend *Morning Crafts* and his other novels highly enough.

Counter-Currents, August 1, 2013

TURNING THE WORLD AROUND:
TITO PERDUE'S *THE NODE*

Tito Perdue
The Node
Charleston, W.V.: Nine-Banded Books, 2011

Tito Perdue's *The Node* is a futuristic, dystopian satire on our anti-white system with an explicitly White Nationalist and New Rightist message.

Satire is easy—just pick a few trends and extrapolate to absurdity. Any idiot can do that, and quite a few have. Which, of course, means that *good* satire is hard to do and hard to find. *The Node*, however, is satire of the highest order: a richly textured, endlessly imaginative, and unfailingly funny vision of a future we are working to avoid. There are surprises and delights on every page. But, like any important discovery or work of the imagination, what seems surprising at first glance seems inevitable upon reflection.

The world of *The Node* is our world, around the middle of this century when whites will become a minority, unless we do something to stop it. Political correctness, anti-white discrimination, feminism, and the unchecked immigration and reproduction of non-whites are rampant. Whites as a race are being replaced by prolific non-whites. White men are being socially displaced by white women. Men are infantilized and emasculated. Women are "strong," which means loud and vulgar, as well as petty and tyrannical.

Society is all about providing equality and inclusion for under-represented, historically marginalized groups, which means: everybody but white men. But instead of creating a utopia of equality and inclusion, society is rigidly hierarchical, with the highest positions awarded to the people with the most defects and the least to offer, people who seethe with neurotic resentment even as they wallow in unearned privileges. White men, being the bottom of the social hierarchy, are subjected to countless indignities by their social superiors.

Fashions are grotesque and undignified, involving forms of body modification and mutilation that cannot be discarded when they go out of style. Expressive individualism reigns, and everyone must conform to its dictates. Pop singers, athletes, and politicians are revered, especially if they are non-white. Sexual promiscuity and perversion are lionized. Literature is crap, but people don't read anyway. They instead watch televised sports and tendentious propaganda dramas. Music is just insolent noise.

Although the cultural sphere is entirely Leftist, the economic system is hyper-oligarchical and capitalist. Nature has been ravaged by pollution: the weather is colder; sunlight is lethal; countless species are extinct. The US has an essentially Third World economy, spewing out cheap plastic junk for vulgar morons. The dollar is worthless, and the currency of choice is the Chinese yuan. The endless, sprawling cities are filthy, impoverished, racially and ethnically segmented, crime-ridden, and chaotic. The United States is still bogged down in senseless wars and police actions around the globe. Still, it's all supposed to be "good for the economy," as the characters never tire of reminding us.

The Node is unique among Perdue's seven published novels because it is not part of the metanarrative of Lee Pefley, the author's semi-autobiographical alter ego. Instead, the nameless 44-year-old protagonist of *The Node* is simply referred to as "our boy" or "the novice." One day, he wanders off his Tennessee farm after a few years of seclusion—during which things have gotten dramatically worse—and ends up in the city. There he happens upon a "node": a fortified enclave of racially-conscious "cauks" (Caucasians) who have banded together for mutual aid and defense and something more.

Nodes, of course, are parts of networks, and the ultimate aim of the network is to "turn the world around," i.e., to establish a white homeland in North America, where our race can perpetuate itself and white civilization can be preserved and perhaps even revivified. As the term "novice" hints, the Nodes are organized as a hierarchical, initiatic, quasi-religious order. The Nodes were created by a very different St. Benedict, "the Master," Larry Schneider, for very different ends. The Nodes thus combine the culturally preservationist function of the rustic Academy of *Morning Crafts* with specifically political, even revolutionary aims.

Schneider's emphasis on high culture and genetic and cultural diversity have an unmistakably "New Right" air. He foresees "a globe of a hundred thousand societies, each following a trajectory of its own, and each becoming more and more unique as time goes on. Diversity I call it" (p. 241). Schneider does not, however, envision peaceful coexistence with the current system, but he thinks that peace is overrated and that the best moral qualities of a people are stirred by war or its moral equivalent.

Education and high culture should be the preserves of the intellectual and creative elites, not dumbed down for the masses, who are more interested in material than spiritual existence. As in *Morning Crafts* and his other books, Perdue believes that the good for all men rests on the foundation of Hobbit-like material comfort, emphasizing wholesomeness, simplicity, and craftsmanship. Some build lives of the mind upon these foundations, but most do not. Since the cultured can appreciate the simple life, but simple people cannot appreciate higher culture, political power should be concentrated in the hands of the cultured and wise for the good of all.

The portrayal of the Nodists is a wry satire on White Nationalists and racially-aware conservatives. At 44, "our boy" is a young whipper-snapper. Most of the other Nodists are old men who combine awareness of the most important matter of all—the threat to our race and what is necessary to preserve it—with various forms of antiquarianism and crankery. There are few women, even fewer nubile and attractive ones, which is a constant source of friction among the men, who naturally think and talk about reproducing with them, but never get around to it. Naturally, the Nodists are a product of the society they wish to destroy, often displaying shocking degrees of indoctrination and bad taste, not to mention alcoholism, loutishness, and unreliability, which must be compassionately indulged to attain their aims—and suppressed if they interfere.

The plot of the novel is rather simple: after a period of education at the Node, our boy leads a number of Nodists into the wilderness to establish a new Node, his travels providing us with a guided tour of dystopia and a few lessons in leadership and community building. As in *Morning Crafts,* Perdue quite casually indicates that a certain amount of ruthlessness and force may be necessary and therefore justified to save our race. If that end does not justify the means, what else could?

The science-fiction elements of *The Node* are handled in a particularly droll way. A device called the "escrubilator" is casually mentioned on practically every page, but it is never really defined or described. It seems to be a weapon as well as a telephone; they are machines, but they also seem to have minds of their own. They go through as many real and specious permutations and upgrades as cell phones, until the whole technology is recalled and, well, scrubbed.

The most amusing trait of the escrubilator is that the

reader simply cannot form a picture of it. It is as unrepresentable as the incident in Gogol's "The Nose," when the protagonist sees his nose leaving town disguised as a civil servant. "Gun porn" being one of the more tiresome traits of Right-wing novels, we should be grateful that the unrepresentability of the escrubilator makes "escrubilator porn" impossible. Although at one point, the protagonist discovers that some escrubilators have crept off do to naughty things in private.

I highly recommend *The Node*. At 258 pages, it is a quick, highly-entertaining read. Perdue's wry humor had me smiling at every page, with an average of one audible laugh every seven pages: all told, an excellent return on my $12.

Tito Perdue is our finest living novelist, proof positive that the tradition of visionary Right-wing fiction that includes D. H. Lawrence, Knut Hamsun, and Wyndham Lewis lives on. *The Node*, like all good satire, is a deeply life-affirming piece of literature, for if we can laugh at evil, we have already defeated it, in our own minds at least.

Counter-Currents, August 16, 2013

THE CULTURED THUG:
TITO PERDUE'S *REUBEN*

> "Truthfully, in this age those with intellect have no courage and those with some modicum of physical courage have no intellect. If things are to alter during the next fifty years then we must re-embrace Byron's ideal: the cultured thug."
>
> —Jonathan Bowden[1]

Tito Perdue
Reuben
Second Edition
Brent, Alabama: Standard American Publishing Company, 2022

Tito Perdue is America's greatest living novelist, and *Reuben* is my favorite of his works. *Reuben* is a satirical meditation on the fallen state of white America and how a white vanguard might be organized to turn the world around. The story begins when a thug named Reuben chances upon a teacher, Tito Perdue's alter ego Lee Pefley, who fashions him into a cultured thug and a man of destiny. *Reuben* is a masterful piece of writing, moving effortlessly between mythic, epic, and satirical modes. It is also highly entertaining and thought-provoking, with biting humor and arresting turns of phrase on every page.

Perdue's novels fall into three rough categories. The first are quasi-autobiographical novels on the life, afterlife,

---

[1] Jonathan Bowden, "Why I Write," in *Pulp Fascism: Right-Wing Themes in Comics, Graphic Novels, & Popular Literature*, ed. Greg Johnson (San Francisco: Counter-Currents, 2013), p. 166.

and antecedents of Lee Pefley, who is Perdue's literary alter-ego. This category includes *Lee* (1991), *The New Austerities* (1994; second edition, 2023), *Opportunities in Alabama Agriculture* (1994; second edition, 2023), *The Sweet-Scented Manuscript* (2004), *Fields of Asphodel* (2007; second edition, 2023), *Morning Crafts* (2013), the *William's House* quartet (2016), *Though We Be Dead, Yet Our Day Will Come* (2018), *The Smut Book* (2018), and *Materials for All Future Historians* (2020).

Cynosura (2017) and *The Philatelist* (2018) belong to their own class, although one can argue that even their main characters are alter-egos of the author.

The third category, comprising *Reuben* plus *The Node* (2011), *Philip* (2017), *The Bent Pyramid* (2018), *The Gizmo* (2019), and *Love Song of the Australopiths* (2020), are Perdue's novels about "turning the world around," the literal meaning of "revolution" in the cultural and political realms.

These books feature secret societies of disproportionately old and cranky individuals dedicated to reversing the decline of white civilization by both preserving books and culture and by accumulating money, which they cash in for political power as well as for new technologies, which in turn they cash in for even more money and political power.

The division between the Pefley novels and the political novels is not air-tight, since Lee makes appearances in *The Bent Pyramid, Philip,* and *Reuben*. In *Reuben*, he plays an especially important role in Book I as the teacher of the title character.

In its ambitions and outline, *Reuben* resembles another novel written by an intellectual who wanted to turn the world around: *Émile* by Jean-Jacques Rousseau. Like *Émile, Reuben* is named for its main character, who is the pupil of a revolutionary intellectual who is the *alter ego* of the author. Like Émile, Reuben is more a child of nature than of the reigning society, which makes them both relatively blank slates for their preceptors' designs. The goal of both preceptors is to make their students as unfit as possible for the society around them and as powerful as necessary to change their societies to fit them. They are new men who will create and set the norms for new societies. The chief way in which *Reuben* departs from *Émile* is by actually showing the pupil revolutionizing the world.

Why are revolutionary intellectuals like Perdue and Rousseau drawn to the problem of education? A revolutionary's task is daunting, and the more radical his program, the more dauting the task. How does one overthrow errors and follies that have reigned for thousands of years? The task seems a little less daunting, however, when one realizes that *even the most ancient traditions live on only in the minds of our contemporaries. Thus, if traditions are not passed on by the present generation, they will die out.* Thus the problem of fundamental cultural and political revolution reduces to a matter of education, and we can do something about that.

THE PHILOSOPHY

Lee was a great admirer of ancient Greece, which prized excellence above equality and thus reposed power in the hands of the best. His enemy was modern egalitarianism, which empowered the masses, who promptly delivered society into the hands of those who are merely rich, not virtuous. Lee asks Reuben:

> Do you sincerely believe that high things are high, and low things low, and higher is better, and all men are utterly unequal? And do you adore what has been done in Europe and especially Greece? And that power properly belongs to those only who have no peers? (ch. 7)

The modern value system is precisely the inverse: "they adore what is weak and dread what is strong" (ch. 27).

Lee's goal, therefore, was to overthrow the modern and postmodern value systems (moral, political, and aesthetic) and restore the classical one. He wished to bequeath to future generations "a world of tremendous inequality where love and art can flourish" (ch. 15). This society would be "designed to foster genius and excellence as opposed to simple happiness understood as an impossible and unworthy ambition" (ch. 27). "He wanted a crystalline civilization in which shallowness were an actionable offense, a society that makes demands upon people and where beauty was to be pursued at any cost you'd care to name. A high culture . . . all white. With intimidating laws and a trajectory all its own" (ch. 24).

Lee wasn't a complete reactionary. He embraced modern science and technology. But he wished to infuse them with archaic moral and aesthetic values. In Guillaume Faye's terms, he was an archeofuturist. For instance, he envisioned a society in which the productivity gains of technological progress would be taken not in the form of more wealth but of more leisure: He "wanted a delimited country with impenetrable tariffs, a lower standard of living, more modest homes, shorter working hours" (ch. 24). It was also important to "keep the wealth out of ignorant hands" (ch. 12).

Lee did, however, think that the scale of modern, globbal society was too large. Thus he wished to "break the cities into towns" (ch. 12).

In sum, both Lee and Reuben "wanted a small country getting smaller, fine people getting finer, a crystalline civilization of earnest people never so far from libraries and opera houses that they couldn't walk" (ch. 30).

THE MAN OF DESTINY

Lee loved history but hated how it turned out. Thus he was ever vigilant for "a chance to turn the course of events around" (p. 28). When Reuben came into his life, he saw such a chance, and took it.

Reuben is a hillbilly, but he is also a genius. He is described as handsome, brawny, and 6 feet 6 inches tall. His physicality is an important part of the package. He is a spectacle, a "monster." His pure physicality allows him to dominate space and cow weaker minds.

But Reuben is far from perfect. He has a lower leg where the flesh has been shorn away in some sort of farm accident. Reuben's imperfection is necessary for his greatness. Had he been perfect, our society would have seduced him into wasting his time and brilliant intellect as a football-playing, womanizing lout. Reuben's wound keeps him somewhat aloof from the rest of humanity, especially women, and thus focused on Lee's mission. It is the heel that allows him to become an Achilles.

As we learn, Lee had found other students, but Reuben was the last and greatest and the man who got it done.

When Reuben stumbles into Lee's life, Lee quickly divines his natural qualities. But natural gifts are not enough. They must be cultivated. They must be yoked alongside knowledge and infused with prudence and taste. As Lee says, "What we see here in America is the absolute triumph of quantity over quality. And that's why your quality has to be larger than their quantity" (ch. 11).

He has a vast library. He can give Reuben free room and board. He settles the lad in, then pours all this knowledge into him, as well as his sense of mission:

> "Take my youth" said Lee, "and take my books, take my knowledge, and take my hate."
>
> The boy nodded. He held the knife, Lee noted, like a harpoon.
>
> "Take my knife," said Lee one more time, "and drive it up to the hilt in that philosophy there, the one that's stopped our country from becoming like Greece" (ch. 5).

Are you the one for it? To take the Democracy and break it like an egg? It lies in the gutter, boy, the western crown. Will you be him who picks it up? (ch. 9)

As is clear, Lee has more than a little of the one-pointed and self-consuming fanaticism of Captain Ahab.

Reuben also has a natural streak of ruthlessness that Lee prizes and cultivates. As one of Lee's allies says to Reuben, "Far too late in the day for pity, Reuben. Promise me that much at least" (ch. 19). As Reuben entered middle age and his mission unfolded, "he had grown a good deal colder than he used to be, inspired more fear, acted with less compunction, and was accomplishing more than he ever had before" (ch. 28).

THE STATION

After his apprenticeship with Lee, Reuben went out into the big world. Having received a superb liberal education from Lee, Reuben focused his higher education on science, technology, and business, all the better to gain power in late modern society. He soon had profitable patents and lucrative research positions in the private sector, the gains of which he invested prudently. These were his journeyman years, largely solitary and apolitical, focused on building up both himself and his portfolio.

Reuben certainly did not dissipate his time and attention in online chit chat. In this, too, he followed Lee's advice:

"Monkeying with my computer?" said Lee. "Very well. But just remember this, that no one ever attained real power by fooling around with binary things. Oh no, you'll have to do much better than that if you expect to take history in your teeth and turn the world about." (ch. 4)

There was no need to hurry into politics, for, as our author notes, "After a certain time, those with revolutionary potential will naturally begin to recognize each other. They might be in meetings or collide into each other on message boards, or they might be called to one another's attention by personality archetypes exposed on holographic actualizations" (ch. 22).

After a chance meeting with someone who pegged Reuben as "one of Lee's people" (ch. 19), Reuben was introduced to a secret society of reactionaries known as "The Station," the purpose of which was "to turn the world around." The group's strategy was metapolitical, because "the democracy was yet too entrenched and too popular by much" to be attacked directly. But "there might be other ways to bring about the victory of quality over quantity and turn the world around" (ch. 23).

These "other ways" consisted primarily of propaganda and discrete networking and lobbying efforts, to which end the group had amassed "above a billion and a half dollars." In short, The Station had solved the problem of recruiting rich idealists.

The Station's strategy had elements of accelerationism and cynicism. Sometimes they seemed downright Jewish, seeking to profit from the nation's decline:

> In a nation controlled by television the group sought a station of its own able to compete in terms of ignorance and vulgarity with the existing ones. They sought a newspaper, sought also to buy a certain federal representative who was ready he said to turn his back on Ashkenazi money. They sought speakers and performers, pornographic studios, a meth monopoly, a basketball franchise, and hoped to take over an extraordinarily profitable civil rights charity with branches in several countries. (ch. 24)

As one of The Station's members put it, "We'll give 'em every fetish in the book. Snuff films! Twenty hours of professional wrestling every week. You agree don't you Reuben? All the sooner to be done with this interlude in Western history and start anew?" (ch. 26).

Reuben immediately joined The Station. His ability was quickly recognized, and he was given tasks to complete. His hard-work, genius, and ruthlessness were rewarded with advancement. Because he was the best, eventually he became the leader.

THE REVOLUTION

The Station started out as an ethnic mafia—a white ethnic mafia—complete with "made men." But its goal was to become what is now called a "deep state." Not only did The Station broadcast highly profitable propaganda to the world, it also focused on building a network of influence by identifying important people and then converting, buying, or bullying them into compliance.

Once The Station attained sufficient power, it began slowly to implement its policies in the political and cultural realms. At first, nobody knew what was happening.

> The government continued to go through the complicated motions, people continued to vote, and yet not one person in 10,000 realized that a new world was aborning. Farmers continue to harvest, etc. It was in other words an invisible revolution very like the one in Lincoln's time period. For 200 years the country had been ruled by money till along came Reuben and his associates. (ch. 29)

By the time people began noticing that society was improving, the sort of people who would object to such a thing had no power to stop it. America's non-white population was swiftly repatriated. The culture was cleaned up.

Wholesome sexual and family norms were reestablished. Love and beauty flourished. The educational system was thoroughly reformed, it being the key to everything else:

> [Reuben's] real interest of course lay in the higher forms of education, a personal specialty of his based upon his time with Leland. He realized quickly that the country had twelve times more schools and universities than students qualified to use them. . . . Now, almost at once the country became more cheerful, the result of young people rescued from the sneers and curdled sophistication that came from imagining they had acquired an education. (ch. 28)

For Reuben, the ideal deep state was staffed by an elite of people "who could recognize beauty when they saw it." These people would govern as "an austere group denied luxuries or name recognition" (ch. 33). Only a few people even suspected that Reuben "hovered over the three branches of government, not to mention a large fraction of private enterprise" (ch. 31), effecting dramatic changes. He was truly the hidden legislator of mankind.

But of course he faced opposition from equally discrete and far-sighted proponents of the opposite design, from whom he had to fend off the occasional assassin. But he enjoyed such opportunities for "exholstering his .38 and allowing it to bark out loud and clear" (ch. 30). It kept life interesting.

Reuben's power was used overwhelmingly for good purposes. But power corrupts. Thus his plans became ever more megalomaniacal:

> The country was improving and the population getting thinner. . . . In March he reinstituted the traditional watermelon seed spitting contests in

Alabama and then a month later demanded an improvement in the manufacturer of book bindings, of color-coordinated highways made to look like streams of gold, gamma-powered automobiles resembling Spanish galleons, flowering crabapple trees from Maine to Minnesota, radio programs in British voices, Elizabethan clothing, timbered buildings preseeded with honeysuckle vines, music by Debussy and Ravel projected over field and dells, luminescent cattle, magnolia trees articulate in Latin and French, mile-high office buildings composed of amethyst, etc., etc. custom-made women's faces, vacation time on the seas of the Andromedan cluster, unification of the Greek and gothic pantheons. (ch. 32)

I couldn't help but chuckle at the fate of old people under the new order: "As for the old people, they found it far better than golf to be marching forward through woods and field while singing songs of death" (ch. 30).

Long ago, Plato noted that the fusion of wisdom and absolute political power is almost miraculous. An even greater miracle is when such a person manages to make the world a better place. But the greatest miracle of all is if such a person has the wisdom to relinquish absolute power before it corrupts him. Reuben performs all three miracles, renouncing his power in the end. Of course, this was possible because Reuben was not a lone genius. He really did have peers. He emerged from an elite, was sustained by it, and could safely hand power back to it in the end.

Reuben is a highly entertaining novel. It deserves a wide audience. But Tito Perdue would surely be satisfied if it fell into the hands of just one reader, as long as he is the right young thug to turn the world around.

Counter-Currents, June 6, 2024

JOHN KENNEDY TOOLE'S
A CONFEDERACY OF DUNCES

John Kennedy Toole
A Confederacy of Dunces
Foreword by Walker Percy
Baton Rouge: Louisiana State University Press, 1980

A Confederacy of Dunces is one of the greatest comic novels ever written. It takes its name from a line of Swift's which serves as its epigraph: "When a true genius appears in the world, you may know him by this sign, that all the dunces are in confederacy against him."

This has a double meaning. First, it is a reference to the book's main character (he cannot be called a hero) Ignatius J. Riley, who thinks he's a genius oppressed by dunces, but isn't. Second, there is something prophetic about this epigraph, for when John Kennedy Toole put these words to paper, he was a genuine genius leading an apparently charmed life. But great hardships awaited him, delivered by dunces both real and imaginary.

Toole submitted *Confederacy* to Roger Gottlieb at Simon and Schuster. Gottlieb praised the book but urged Toole to revise it, and then revise it again and again. After two years of revisions and correspondence, Toole gave up in frustration and disgust, put the manuscript in a box, and focused on other things. He was a brilliant scholar and teacher and had great prospects as a university professor of English literature.

When Toole was 30, his friends and family started noticing classic symptoms of paranoia. He actually believed that the dunces around him were conspiring against him. Eventually, he emptied his bank account and drove off, abandoning his home, job, and Ph.D. program in New

Orleans. After crisscrossing America for more than two months, Toole committed suicide by gassing himself in his car with exhaust. It was 1969. John Kennedy Toole was 31 years old.

Confederacy was published due to the tireless efforts of Toole's mother Thelma. After the book was passed over by a long list of mainstream publishing dunces, Thelma enlisted novelist Walker Percy, who helped place it at Louisiana State University Press, where it was published in 1980 to enormous critical and commercial acclaim.

Confederacy won the 1981 Pulitzer Prize for fiction and has sold more than two million copies in 23 languages. Even the titles of the translations will make you laugh: *Die Verschwörung der Idioten*, *Una confabulació d'imbècils*, *Uma Conspiração de Estúpidos*, *Dumskallarnas sammansvärjning*, *Fjolsernes forbund*, etc.

Toole was an extraordinary talent, and *Confederacy* is a masterpiece. So why did it take so long to get into print? I think the main reason is that the book is quite politically incorrect. Blacks are depicted as shiftless buffoons. Gay men are depicted as campy, superficial, sex-obsessed pinheads. Lesbians are depicted as boorish brutes. Jews are depicted as rich, neurotic, and obsessed with sex and psychotherapy. Toole's Jewish characters also have strong penchants to meddle—sometimes disastrously—in the lives, culture, and politics of the *goyim*.

In truth, every character in *Confederacy* is some sort of idiot or buffoon, including all the whites, whether they be Irish, Italian, French Creole, or Anglo. But it is okay to mock poor white people, especially in the South. (*Confederacy* is set in New Orleans.) Yet it is not okay to mock blacks, homosexuals, and Jews. Indeed, according to Toole's biographer Cory MacLaughlin, the Jewish characters were a particular sticking point for Roger Gottlieb[1] at

---

[1] Cory MacLauchlin, *Butterfly in the Typewriter: The Tragic*

Simon and Schuster. Given Jewish sensitivities about anti-Semitism, which are also mocked in *Confederacy*, it certainly seems plausible that Jews and non-Jews alike throughout the publishing industry shared the same reservations. Moreover, after *Confederacy* became a bestseller, Thelma Toole explicitly claimed that Jewish ethnic animus played a role in Gottlieb's decision not to publish the book.[2]

A Confederacy of Dunces is the story of Ignatius P. Reilly, the only child of a working class Irish Catholic family in New Orleans. It is set in the early 1960s, when the book was written. The civil rights movement, including Jewish outside agitators, is in the background.

Ignatius is 30, his father is dead, and he lives at home with his mother Irene. Ignatius is the precocious child of ordinary people, which means he was not particularly well-understood by his family and neighbors. He was probably the first generation of his family to go to college. Then he earned a master's degree. Something medieval. He's always bloviating about Boethius and Hrotsvitha of Gandersheim.

But after that something snapped. He couldn't launch. He keeps recounting a traumatic visit to a university in Baton Rouge (perhaps Louisiana State, which eventually published the book). Was he there to interview for a teaching job? Or was he hoping to continue his graduate studies? The answer is not clear. What is clear is that the trip ended in disaster.

Ignatius retreated to his bedroom in New Orleans, where he has stagnated ever since. When we meet him, he is fat, slovenly, and self-indulgent. He spends his time

---

Life of John Kennedy Toole and the Remarkable Story of A Confederacy of Dunces (New York: Da Capo Press, 2012), pp. 174, 241–42.

[2] MacLauchlin, *Butterfly in the Typewriter*, pp. 241–42.

hate-watching movies and television and listening to pop songs. He condemns pop culture as vulgar and decadent but continues to consume it. He scribbles pompous diatribes on children's drawing tablets but never attempts to publish them. He farts around with musical instruments, the more archaic the better (the lute, the recorder). He consumes vast amounts of sweets, soft-drinks, and hot dogs, growing ever fatter.

Ignatius has never had a real girlfriend. He had a pretend girlfriend in Myrna Minkoff, a Jewish Leftist agitator whom he knew in college. But when she tried to consummate things, the neighbor next door could hear Ignatius screaming "Put down that skirt . . . Get off my bed. . . . How dare you? I'm a virgin" (p. 319). Ignatius is, however, a compulsive masturbator, which he turned into something of an art form, even a ritual, involving such accoutrements as a rubber glove, a strip of silk from an old umbrella, and a jar of Noxema (p. 26).

Yet despite his degraded existence, Ignatius speaks pompously and carries himself with great dignity. He is actually an extreme narcissist. Not all narcissists are beautiful people. Ugly and obnoxious people can be narcissists too, but they gain their sense of superiority not by being admired by others, but by holding others in contempt. Ignatius hoists himself up by putting others down. He's rude, obnoxious, and condescending.

Ignatius reconciles his inflated self-image with his squalid existence through an array of postures, excuses, and delusions. Basically, Ignatius tells himself that he fails at life because he's too good for this world.

Ignatius broke with the Catholic church as a teen when a priest refused to officiate at the burial of his dog. But sometimes he finds it convenient to embrace Catholicism in its high medieval form as a perspective from which he can condemn the whole modern world for its "lack of theology and geometry" (p. 1). But of all the things the medievals looked down upon, the only one Ignatius abstains from is work.

Ignatius also embraces a diametrically opposed worldview, modern psychology, for it too provides him with copious excuses for failure. Thus he speaks endlessly of his traumas, which oddly do not motivate him to do something. They function only as excuses for more idleness.

Finally, Ignatius is a hypochondriac, always going on about how emotional upset causes his "valve" to constrict, preventing food from passing from his stomach to his intestine. This must be of special concern to someone who never stops eating.

Ignatius, in short, is one of the first literary appearances of what people on the Alt Right spoke of as the "NEET," a British acronym for "Not in Education, Employment, or Training." If Ignatius were born in the 1990s, he would today be an "extremely online" gamer and "shitposter." He'd still be fat. He'd still be living at home, sponging off his parents. He'd still be a virgin. He'd still be masturbating, but now with a whole world of online porn to consume. He'd still be rude and condescending. And he'd still be pouring scorn down on modernity from on high, although he'd probably be citing Evola alongside Boethius and Hrotsvitha.

Ignatius also appears to be what James O'Meara calls a "Trad Queen": a homosexual who embraces an ultra-traditionalist form of Catholicism as a cover for never having sex with women.[3] But of course Ignatius is too self-indulgent to actually enter the priesthood. Toole doesn't explicitly say that Ignatius is homosexual. In fact, the one sexual fantasy he relates involves a dog (p. 27). But there's definitely something flamboyant about him. Even though he is a disgusting slob, he carries himself grandly and with

---

[3] James J. O'Meara, "Trad Queen Story Hour," parts 1–3, *Counter-Currents*, June 12, 15, and 16, 2020.

his own sort of style. What, for instance, are we to make of Ignatius going on about his muffler to an old man who was considering hiring him as a hotdog vendor?

> ". . . It can also be worn as a shawl. Look."
> "Well," the old man said finally, after watching Ignatius employ the muffler as a cummerbund, a sash, and a pair of kilts, a sling for a broken arm, and a kerchief, "you ain't gonna do too much damage to Paradise Vendors in one hour." (p. 139)

Homosexuals also initially take him for one of their own, although he quickly wears out his welcome because he's too self-absorbed and rude to be any fun.

As the novel progresses, Ignatius' bloated self-image is increasingly punctured and deflated as his deeds come back to haunt him. But as a narcissist, Ignatius is incapable of reflecting on and revising his self-image, thus he reacts with rage and increasing paranoia.

An inflated self-image logically leads to paranoia, for if one thinks too highly of oneself and refuses to revise such views in light of failures and negative feedback, how do you explain why others don't love you as much as you think they should? Malice or stupidity is the most likely explanation. And when many people share the same negative judgments of you, that can't be because they are all based on the same facts, namely your actual negative traits. No, the only possible explanation is that malice and stupidity are passing from person to person like a contagion, i.e., the dunces—*evil* dunces—are in a confederacy against you.

The basic story of *Confederacy* is that Irene Reilly can no longer afford to keep Ignatius in leisure, so she forces him to get a job.

The first job he takes is at the Levy Pants factory, which is run by Gus Levy, a nice guy with a hands-off management style, unlike his shrewish wife, who fancies herself educated because she signed up for a correspondence course in psychology. She has made a hobby of *tikkun olaming* Miss Trixie, their superannuated accountant who is a hoarder and slipping into dementia.

As soon as Ignatius is hired, he begins decorating the office like a kindergarten classroom (anything to avoid work) and plotting against his colleagues. Eventually, he organizes the black laborers into a Crusade for Moorish Dignity and tries to incite a riot. The riot fizzles, and Ignatius is fired.

Ignatius is completely uninterested in progressive political causes. He thinks blacks are childish and primitive but envies what he imagines to be their innocence. He also wishes to weaponize them against the bourgeois society that would force him to work. But his primary motive for organizing the Crusade for Moorish Dignity is merely to impress/show up Myrna Minkoff.

Myrna is modeled after some of Toole's students at Hunter College in the early 1960s, whom he characterized as "aggressive, pseudo-intellectual 'liberal' girls"[4] who, according to his friend Clayelle Dalferes, were "only interested in anti-Semitism."[5] Ever vigilant against antisemitism, Myrna is the epitome of Jewish radicalism. The daughter of a wealthy businessman, she incites blacks against whites and Catholics against WASPs. She is a fervent believer in psychoanalysis as well, preaching personal and political redemption through orgasms. Naturally, she also promotes miscegenation between whites and blacks. Just as Mrs. Levy has adopted Miss Trixie, Myrna has made Ignatius her hobby, her project.

Ignatius' next job is as a hot dog vendor, for which he is ill-suited because he's lazy, churlish, and eats most of the

---

[4] MacLauchlin, *Butterfly in the Typewriter*, p. 112.
[5] MacLauchlin, *Butterfly in the Typewriter*, p. 112.

inventory. Ignatius' employer sends him to the French Quarter to hawk weenies dressed as a pirate. This catches the attention of Dorian Greene, a flamboyant homosexual who invites Ignatius to one of his fabulous parties.

Ignatius plans to use the party to launch a new political movement to Save the World Through Degeneracy. Ignatius wants gay men to infiltrate the highest levels of politics and the military around the world. Once we are ruled by homosexuals, he avers,

> ... the world will enjoy not war but global orgies conducted with the utmost protocol and the most truly international spirit, for these people do transcend simple national differences. Their minds are on one goal; they are truly united; they think as one. ... From time to time the Chief of Staff, the President, and so on, dressed in sequins and feathers, will entertain the leaders, i.e., the perverts, of all the other countries at balls and parties. Quarrels of any sort could easily be straightened out in the men's room of the redecorated United Nations. (pp. 238-39)

Again, Ignatius is not really interested in world peace or gay rights. He's just trying to get a rise out of Myrna Minkoff. She acknowledges that the "Sodomite business" has some merit: "I can see that we might use this Sodomite party to drain off the fringe-group fascists. Maybe we could split the right wing in half" (p. 269). But she's more concerned with Ignatius' mental health. By this time in the novel, the reader has concluded that Ignatius is not just colorful and eccentric, he's insane and malevolent. Myrna, however, thinks he can be saved through "therapy" and recommends that he get it immediately, lest he become a "screaming queen" (p. 269).

Ignatius' attempt to launch the Save the World

Through Degeneracy movement is a predictable flop. The gays just want to chatter, drink cocktails, and listen to Lena Horne. The lesbians just want to smash beer cans on their faces.

After some more misadventures, including being attacked by a parrot from a burlesque show, Ignatius ends up passed out on the streetcar tracks, laid up in the hospital, plastered on the front page of the newspaper, and fired from his vending job.

Irene is mortified. Apparently, the only thing more disgraceful than being a weenie vendor is being in the newspapers. The last straw, however, is not the public disgrace. When Irene wants to remarry in her 50s, Ignatius tries to prevent it. He doesn't care about her happiness. He just wants his mother's undivided attention.

Irene finally realizes she has raised a monster: "You learnt everything, Ignatius, except how to be a human being" (p. 322). She loses all interest in his prattle and decides to have him committed to the psychiatric ward of Charity Hospital, which was a place of horror.

Fortunately for Ignatius, Myrna Minkoff arrives from New York in the nick of time to spirit him away. "This is a very meaningful moment," she says. "I feel as if I am *saving* someone" (p. 345). She has found a new project, and Ignatius has found a new mommy. It isn't long, though, before she has second thoughts: "Ignatius, all at once you're your old horrible self. All at once I think I'm making a very big mistake" (p. 347). But Ignatius manages to allay her fears. The end of the novel is ambiguous:

> He stared gratefully at the back of Myrna's head, at the pigtail that swung innocently at his knee. Grateful. How ironic, Ignatius thought. Taking the pigtail in one of his paws, he pressed it warmly to his wet moustache. (p. 348)

Genuine gratitude is a new experience for Ignatius. But as soon as he thinks it is ironic, he is already distancing himself from it. His old horrible self will soon be making a comeback.

Nevertheless, if you read this novel, you will be dying to know what happens next. Then you will die a little when you remember that there was no next chapter in Ignatius' life, or in the life of his creator.

Confederacy has been criticized for being "plotless" and "about nothing." Of course such trifles never stopped *Seinfeld* from being hilarious. But these accusations are unjust. *Confederacy* has a number of concurrent plotlines with overlapping characters that weave in and out of each other in a fugal fashion.

Toole also includes recurring themes, like Wagnerian *Leitmotives*, which recur with perfect comic timing. The most hilarious is Ignatius' valve. Others include Mrs. Levy's exercise table, Miss Trixie's dentures, and Burma Jones' clouds of smoke.

Confederacy is less like a movie with a unified plot than a situation comedy series. In fact, although all attempts to adapt it to the screen have failed, *Confederacy* would make a great miniseries of about six to eight episodes. Larry David would be the perfect director.

Critics also condemn *Confederacy* because the characters don't change. This is unjust too. First, some of the characters do change. Chief among them is Ignatius' mother, Irene, who finally decides to stop indulging her son and start enjoying what's left of her own life. Mr. Levy changes by deciding finally to make his father's business his own and to cast off his nagging, malevolent wife. Even Ignatius seems to change a little bit at the very end. But his chances remain quite slim. Second, Toole believed that people don't *really* change. They just become more themselves.

Although Toole was an admirer of Flannery O'Connor

and was himself brought up Catholic, *Confederacy* does not have an O'Connoresque "moment of grace," where God intervenes in human life. This is also true of Toole's other novel, *The Neon Bible*, an astonishingly mature work that Toole wrote at the age of 16, very much under O'Connor's influence.

Inevitably, people wonder if Ignatius is based on a real person. One source was Bobby Byrne, an English professor at the University of Southwestern Louisiana, where Toole taught for a year. Byrne inspired Ignatius' general build, voice, and manner, as well as his absurd style of dress, his musical hobbies, and his interest in the Middle Ages.

But the deeper inspiration came from Toole himself. Like Ignatius, Toole was an Irish Catholic from New Orleans, an only child, and an intellectual with a Masters' Degree. Toole had a tendency toward fatness, but he kept the weight off until he began descending into madness. He wasn't homosexual, but he was sometimes thought to be. Ignatius is insane, with a strong paranoid streak. There was insanity on both sides of Toole's family, and it claimed him in the end.

But Ignatius is not Toole's self-portrait. (Nor is Irene a portrait of Toole's mother Thelma. There is almost no resemblance.) Ignatius Reilly is a portrait of a vice-ridden and ultimately insane pseudo-intellectual crank. The portrait has a "There but for the grace of God go I" quality, because Toole constructed Ignatius by first imagining himself and then subtracting all his virtues. (Flannery O'Connor's scathing portraits of intellectuals were constructed in the exact same way.)

Toole was a serious intellectual. A child prodigy, he skipped two grades in elementary school, entered Tulane at 16, graduated with honors, then completed his master's degree in literature at Columbia in one year, graduating with high honors. He was a highly talented and popular teacher at the University of Southwestern Louisiana, at

Hunter College, in the US Army, and at Dominican College in New Orleans. Ignatius, by contrast, is a dilettante and crank. Toole was enormously industrious and well-organized. Ignatius is lazy and chaotic. Toole was highly sociable, mixed well with all sorts of people, and was a meticulous observer of human nature and behavior, all of which is reflected in his novels. Ignatius, however, is entirely self-absorbed and alien to humanity. Toole was known for his gallant Southern manners. He was a sharp dresser, a good dancer, and the life of any party: charming, witty, and a gifted mimic. Ignatius is a slovenly boor. Toole was heterosexual and popular with women. Ignatius is a virgin and a likely homosexual. Toole actually supported his parents financially when they fell on hard times. Ignatius is a parasite on his mother. By all accounts, Toole was well aware of his gifts, but he was empathetic and ethical in his dealings with others—although people feared becoming the butt of his jokes and mimicry. Ignatius, however, is just a mean and selfish bastard.

This brings us to another sense in which *Confederacy* is politically incorrect. We are ruled by people who think of themselves as intellectuals. The publishing industry is certainly full of them. Toole created a scathing satire of a pseudointellectual and offered it as a mirror. Many readers winced and quietly marked Toole as a traitor to their class. Radical political movements are also havens for pompous pseudo-intellectuals and cranks. We need to know how to spot them before they become ensconced. Thus I recommend *A Confederacy of Dunces* highly, not just as a literary masterpiece but as a diagnostic tool. You'll laugh a whole lot. But sometimes you might be laughing at yourself.

Counter-Currents, November 14, 2024

BILL HOPKINS' *THE LEAP!*

Bill Hopkins
The Leap!
Foreword by Colin Wilson
London: Deverell & Birdsey, 1984

Bill Hopkins (1928–2011) was a British Right-wing writer and intellectual who was associated in the 1950s with the so-called Angry Young Men, which was less a movement than a loose journalistic appellation for writers from mostly working- and middle-class backgrounds who were dubbed "angry" because of their disillusionment with post-World War II British society. Some of the Angries hardly knew each other.

In 1957, Hopkins' first novel, *The Divine and the Decay*, was published in London by MacGibbon & Kee.[1] Also in 1957, MacGibbon & Kee published his manifesto, "Ways Without a Precedent," in *Declaration*,[2] an anthology of the Angry Young Men, along with contributions by Colin Wilson, Stuart Holroyd, Lindsay Anderson, Kenneth Tynan, John Osborne, and others, including Doris Lessing, who was neither young nor angry, and was also a woman.

It was a promising start. Many of Hopkins' fellow Angries went on to enjoy outstanding careers. Anderson was an award-winning film, television, and theatre director, as well as a critic. His best-known movie is *If . . .* (1968). Tynan enjoyed success as a theatre critic and writer, best known for some filth called *Oh! Calcutta!* (1969). Osborne was a playwright, screenwriter, and actor best known for

---

[1] Bill Hopkins, *The Divine and the Decay* (London: MacGibbon & Kee, 1957).

[2] Bill Hopkins, "Ways Without a Precedent," in *Declaration*, ed. Tom Maschler (London: MacGibbon & Kee, 1957).

Look Back in Anger (1956). Wilson published more than 100 books. Holroyd too became a prolific author. (The odd girl out, Lessing, wrote more than 50 novels. She won the Nobel Prize in Literature in 2007—and actually deserved it.)

Hopkins' career, however, was cut short by the storm of criticism that greeted *The Divine and the Decay*, which was condemned not just as bad writing but as a danger to liberal democracy.[3] To protect human rights and impressionable youth, Hopkins' publisher decided to withdraw and pulp all unsold copies, even though the book was enjoying respectable sales not merely despite but because of the critical furor.

Hopkins never accepted the judgment of his critics, of course, but the experience was still demoralizing. When the manuscript of his second novel, *Time of Totality*, was accidentally destroyed by a cigarette, Hopkins did not bother to retype it.[4] Instead, Hopkins became a successful art and antiques dealer. He disappeared so completely from the literary scene that Doris Lessing thought that he had died young.[5]

In 1984, *The Divine and the Decay* was republished as *The Leap!* by a London-based firm called Deverell & Birdsey. Hopkins' faithful friend Colin Wilson penned a Foreword. This time, however, the book went almost unnoticed. If the first edition was aborted, the second was stillborn.

When it comes to literature, I never read bad books. I admit that I have *started* many of them. But as soon as it

---

[3] I am drawing upon Colin Wilson's *The Angry Years: The Rise and Fall of the Angry Young Men* (London: Robson Books, 2007), pp. 126–30.

[4] Wilson, *The Angry Years*, p. 130.

[5] Jonathan Bowden, "Bill Hopkins' *The Divine and the Decay*," *Western Civilization Bites Back*, ed. Greg Johnson (San Francisco: Counter-Currents, 2014), p. 158.

becomes clear that a book is bad, I toss it aside. Life is just too short for bad books. I have read *The Leap!* twice, which means that I think it is a good book. But if I am reading *The Leap!* correctly, I must conclude that everyone else has gotten it wrong: not just the critics but Hopkins himself, as well as his friends Colin Wilson and Jonathan Bowden, even the redoubtable Revilo P. Oliver.[6]

To a man, they all see Peter Plowart, the main character of *The Leap!*, as an earnest portrait of a Nietzschean *Übermensch* who aspires to dictatorial power and is willing to wade through oceans of blood to attain it. This sent Hopkins' critics into paroxysms of rage while spurring his friends to admiration and apologetics.

But I read *The Leap!* as a darkly comic depiction of a man who is both loathsome and laughable. Plowart is a narcissistic sociopath. He has delusions of grandeur. He thinks of himself as a great man, a man of destiny. He also thinks himself far cleverer than he actually is. Moreover, he repeatedly sabotages himself through arrogance, impulsiveness, and downright stupidity.

The Leap! is genuinely comic, but darkly comic, because Plowart leaves a wake of misery and death behind him. He may well die in the end. Hopkins leaves that unclear. But if he does survive, it is by sheer luck and the connivance of another piece of human dross.

The Leap! is ideal material for a Coen Brothers film in the vein of *Blood Simple* or *Fargo*. Many episodes of the plot are farcical, featuring a cheating wife, a jealous drunken husband, even a lover climbing into a window with a rope and grappling hook. Midway in the novel, Hopkins introduces a letter confessing to a shocking murder. This letter is stolen, then retrieved, then stolen again, then used as blackmail to arrange a sexual encounter

---

[6] Revilo P. Oliver, "Bill Hopkins' *The Divine and the Decay*," *Counter-Currents*, June 7, 2011.

(employing the aforementioned rope and grapple), then retrieved through another murder. No, Plowart does not drop an anvil on the victim's head.

The Leap! is set in Britian in the 1950s. Peter Plowart is the second-in-command of a Right-wing political party, the New Britain League. On the eve of an election, he decides to murder the party leader, Sir Gregory Bourcey, and take control. He finds someone to commit the crime. Then, to give himself an alibi, he travels to the fictional isle of Vachau, in the Channel Islands.

This is a hare-brained scheme. Because Plowart has arranged the murder, presumably he can arrange the time. Thus he can provide himself with an alibi anywhere, simply by being with someone at the time of the crime. And wouldn't it be better to be with people who knew him, rather than strangers who might take no notice of him? Beyond that, simply having an alibi is not sufficient to clear one of involvement if one had partners in crime.

Being a narcissist, Plowart is the kind of man who walks into a room and immediately sizes up everyone in terms of a hierarchy: some are to be sucked up to; most are to be shat down upon. This, he tells himself, is the Nietzschean way: will-to-power and all that.

But that's just a rationalization for a self-defeating psychological compulsion to gain attention for himself by causing pain in others. Beautiful and charming narcissists attract admiration by being beautiful and charming. Ugly and disagreeable narcissists attract attention by being obnoxious. Everywhere Plowart goes, he takes pleasure in making others uncomfortable, even if it is merely by being a surly conversationalist. *Nota bene*: If you want to gain power, shouldn't you be concerned with making friends rather than enemies everywhere you go?

Despite his conviction of superiority, Plowart's obnoxious behavior is rooted in an inferiority complex. He is convinced that he will fail in every relationship, so he destroys them in advance in order to maintain a sense of control. Convinced that he is doomed to lose, he resolves at least to lose on his own terms.[7]

Because Plowart decided to go to Vachau for his alibi, he can't easily keep abreast of the news, especially news of his crime. Thus he takes a short-wave radio with him. When the radio is accidentally broken on the journey, he flies into a rage and slaps the man who bumped it. When the man and his friends threaten retaliation, Plowart draws a knife. Who are these peasants to get in his way? Why should he treat them any better than a dog he might kick in the street? But it turns out that all three are among the 70 residents of Vachau. He'll be seeing more of them. *Nota bene*: If you are trying to establish your alibi for an upcoming murder for which you will be a person of interest, it is best not to act like a violent psychopath in public.

Plowart then takes great pains to get his radio fixed. When this proves impossible, he seeks out a place on Vachau where he can listen to the radio the next day. It is only after he hears of Bourcey's murder the following morning that he begins to think that he has shown a bit too much interest in listening to the news, something that practically everyone he has encountered could testify to, along with his violent temper. What a brilliant alibi this genius has woven for himself.

When Plowart arrives on Vachau, the natives already know who he is and give him a chilly reception. When an outcast named Buffonet carries Plowart's luggage for money, he is beaten for breaking ranks. Fortunately, Plowart is not the only outsider on the island. He stays in the house of a crippled English drunkard named Lumas and his unfaithful local wife. The host installs Plowart in an attic room, accessible only by a ladder. This is the room

---

[7] Greg Johnson, "Honorable Defeatists," *In Defense of Prejudice* (San Francisco: Counter-Currents, 2017).

used by his wife and her lover for their assignations, since the cripple cannot climb the ladder. As soon as he sets foot in his new room, Plowart tears down the pictures and tears up the rugs. Beyond creating conflict, what is the point of such behavior? He's only a temporary resident. When Mrs. Lumas asks Plowart to change rooms (because her lover will soon visit), he haughtily refuses, deepening her resentment. This pointlessly boorish behavior will soon have consequences, as everyone but a Nietzschean *Übermensch* could predict.

A police detective is sent to interview Plowart about his comrade's death. As a general rule, detectives love criminals with highly inflated egos: medical doctors, college professors, your garden variety *Übermensch*. They are never as clever as they think they are, so it is child's play to catch them lying. Plowart is arrogant and evasive. In the first few seconds, he establishes himself as the prime suspect by pretending to be surprised at the news of Bourcey's death, even though the locals—and thus the detective—know that he already heard the news, even though he has already written and posted statements on Bourcey's death.

Plowart is later told that a letter has come for him from the mainland, but the detective has intercepted it. Plowart demands the letter before the detective has a chance to open it. When he reads it, he is thunderstruck. Plowart the genius apparently chose complete imbeciles to kill Bourcey. They were supposed to make it look like a robbery gone wrong, but they forgot to steal anything. Plowart has a nasty temper, so to placate him, one of the imbeciles sat down and wrote a letter of apology detailing the entire murder and incriminating both of them in the process.

Later Mrs. Lumas' brutish lover Lachanell gives Plowart a well-deserved beating and steals the letter. But he too is an imbecile. When he reads the letter, his first thought is not to protect his lover from the homicidal psychopath staying in her house. Instead, he uses the letter to blackmail Plowart so he no longer prevents him from visiting Mrs. Lumas. Plowart, however, lures Lachanell into a trap and incites the drunken Mr. Lumas to attack him. Lachanell is stabbed, maybe even killed, and the incriminating letter is recovered and burned. Hopkins' description of how Plowart hatches this scheme is telling: Plowart spends a morning chain-smoking and getting staggering drunk on rum. This is typical sociopath behavior. Shallow emotions lead to easy boredom. Boredom leads to the pursuit of easy stimulation through drugs and alcohol.

The most remarkable resident of Vachau is a young woman, Claremont Capothy, the daughter of the Island's Seigneur. (Vachau is modeled on Sark, which had a feudal form of government until 2008, when it was ended due to the connivance of the European Union and the billionaire Barclay brothers.) Claremont is highly intelligent, psychologically insightful, and entirely self-possessed. She immediately sees through Plowart's façade of self-confidence and superiority. He is crippled by an inner emptiness and tormented by nightmares. The inner emptiness is his lack of a soul, i.e., empathy for others, hence his lack of conscience and estrangement from humanity, which he mistakes for superiority. Her diagnosis of Plowart is: ". . . fear is your strongest characteristic, and you can only go forward by a desperate explosion of will."[8]

Plowart is drawn to Claremont because he wants to know the secret of her self-possession. She is also a beautiful young woman. And, being a narcissist, he needs an audience. Unfortunately, since Plowart is a phony, he needs an audience of people he can fool, which simply adds to his loneliness. He seems to fool nobody but himself, but after a few moments, most people give him a wide berth,

---

[8] *The Leap!*, p. 53.

so he persists in his delusion of superiority. He is in the pit of hell but thinks he is just lonely at the top.

Claremont proves to be a dangerously perceptive audience. After just a few minutes of Plowart's Nietzschean posturing, she intuits that he was behind Bourcey's murder. When she asks him flat-out, his reaction is damning. You'd think a genius would have anticipated such a possibility. Plowart's lack of empathy made it possible for him to commit murder. His narcissism makes it impossible for him to keep it a secret. Also, his lack of empathy guarantees that his attempts to manipulate others are clumsy and obvious to normal people.

In the absence of her father, the Seigneur, Claremont is the law on Vachau. But instead of arresting Plowart, she tries to help him. Clearly she is smitten. Claremont is drawn to Plowart because, like so many women, she initially mistakes his Dark Triad traits—narcissism, sociopathy, and would-be Machiavellianism (as we see, his schemes are pathetically clumsy and self-defeating)—as healthy "Alpha" traits. Hopkins does not really describe Plowart's appearance but does mention that he has a superb physique, which can't hurt.

The two have a brief but complicated relationship. When Plowart tries to rape her, she stops him cold by displaying her naked body, which is beautiful, but the gesture destroys his ardor. Later, she invites him to stay over at the Seigneury, which leads to what Ayn Rand called "rape by engraved invitation." Claremont's superior self-possession, however, leaves Plowart feeling empty and humiliated. But when Plowart gleefully outlines how he incited Lumas to assault and likely murder his wife's lover, Claremont decides that Plowart cannot be helped. Instead, he must die.

Claremont tells Plowart that the secret of her self-possession is a quasi-mystical experience she had when she swam to some rocks off Vachau through a swift and deadly current. At a certain point, as she crossed the dangerous waters, "the rocks moved" toward her.

What she means by this is unclear. Did the current suddenly shift? Or did she overcome the currents and her fear "by a desperate explosion of will"?

Maybe she never swam to the rocks at all. Maybe she is trying to lure Plowart to certain death. Or maybe she is just trying to test him by putting him in a dangerous situation. (Something she has already done in the novel.)

Claremont joins him in the swim. If the swim is impossible, then she is killing herself. If the swim is possible, then she still may be counting on her superior skills to save her while the currents rid the world of Plowart.

Whatever her intent, the whole idea seems harebrained. Wouldn't it have been simpler to just call the police? This sequence, moreover, is the climax of the novel. This is a serious dramatic flaw that I first encountered in *A Passage to India*. One should never make the climax of a story contingent on an inscrutable twist or kink of feminine psychology.

Claremont is swept away, probably to her doom. Plowart, however, has that "desperate explosion of will." "The rocks move." Exhausted, he manages to clamber upon them to safety.

When Claremont and Plowart plunge into the dangerous waters, a local sounds the alarm, and a rescue boat is launched. When the rescue boat arrives at the rocks, it is captained by Quiller, the local whom Plowart slapped and threatened with a knife for accidentally breaking his radio. Quiller decides to leave Plowart to the elements for allowing Claremont to drown, as well as for being an all-round bastard.

As the boat turns away, Plowart begins shouting, "You can't kill me, you fools! I'm indestructible, I tell you . . ."[9]

---

[9] *The Leap!*, p. 234.

This is the precise opposite of what he should say. I am sure Plowart's delusions of grandeur are sincere. But in truth, he's on the brink of destruction, his life is entirely in Quiller's hands, and a bit of contrition is his only rational hope. But Plowart is so detached from reality that he can't even lie to save his life.

However, as the boat moves off, one of the men on board slyly releases a life preserver. It is Buffonet, the outcast. It is never made clear if Plowart finds the life preserver or reaches shore. But he continues his insulting harangue. The last words of the novel are: "Indestructible, you fools!"

You'd need a heart of stone not to find this funny.

The critics of *The Leap!* evidently thought that Hopkins wished to depict Peter Plowart as a hero to be emulated. Thus the book had to be stopped, first by bad reviews then by being pulled from publication.

My defense is that *The Leap!* is obviously a satire, that Plowart is not a hero but a buffoon, that no intelligent reader could admire or imitate him, and that Hopkins' liberal critics should be deeply satisfied that Plowart gets his comeuppance in the end.

But this was not the defense offered by Hopkins or his po-faced friends Wilson and Bowden. Moreover, as the careers of various Alt-Right Plowarts prove, there is no shortage of people who will follow transparent narcissists and sociopaths, sticking with them through self-induced crisis after self-induced crisis and never getting the joke.

In a way, it is fortunate that the Right seems to attract only Dark Dyad types: narcissistic sociopaths who are so inept at Machiavellianism that they are incapable of concealing their repulsive traits and reining in their self-destructive impulses. True Dark Triad types would be harder to spot and thus far more damaging. But they probably gravitate toward mainstream politics, where the real money and power are.

So maybe *The Leap!* is only a comedy by accident. Maybe it really is a dangerous book. But if Hopkins' portrait of Peter Plowart can inoculate readers against falling for real-life versions, you may find the *The Leap!* worth diving into.

Counter-Currents, January 30, 2024

Superheroes, Sovereignty, & the Deep State

The superhero genre in comics and movies was largely created by Jews.[1] In some of my writings on film, I have argued that superheroes largely function as symbolic proxies for Jews.[2] Superheroes, like Jews, are outsiders and "freaks." They are, moreover, immensely powerful outsiders. Thus, lest they incite the fear and ire of their host populations, they must practice crypsis to blend in.

Superheroes also play an apologetic role for Jewry. Despite near total Jewish hegemony in the media and educational system, the public mind is still aware of stories of secret Jewish cabals plotting to harm the *goyim*, from the Elders of Zion to the Project for a New American Century and the Office of Special Plans. Thus, to immunize the public from automatically regarding such cabals with suspicion, the superhero genre portrays these immensely powerful and secretive outsiders—individually, and in groups like the Justice League, the X-Men, and the Avengers—as committed to the morality of egalitarian humanism and benevolently serving the interests of humanity.

Of course, in reality the Bolsheviks, neocons, and their like more closely resemble supervillains than superheroes.

---

[1] See Ted Sallis' review of *From Krakow to Krypton: Jews & Comic Books*, *Counter-Currents*, October 12, 2011.

[2] See my reviews of *Hellboy* and *Hellboy II: The Golden Army* in *Trevor Lynch's White Nationalist Guide to the Movies*, ed. Greg Johnson, Foreword by Kevin MacDonald (San Francisco: Counter-Currents, 2012) and *Man of Steel* in *Son of Trevor Lynch's White Nationalist Guide to the Movies*, ed. Greg Johnson (San Francisco: Counter-Currents, 2015).

Superheroes, Sovereignty, & the Deep State

Thus, to inoculate the public mind from drawing that sort of conclusion, supervillains are usually portrayed as Nazis, or symbolic proxies for Nazis. Basically, supervillains are illiberal, elitist, and nationalistic, with traditional or archaic rather than modern values, whereas superheroes are liberal, globalist, and devoted to serving their inferiors.

But superheroes can exemplify Right-wing political themes as well. I want to argue that superheroes are the fictional genre that best illustrates Carl Schmitt's antiliberal concept of sovereignty. Specifically, I wish to speak about the masked vigilante genre, epitomized by Batman, in which accomplished but still biologically human individuals use criminal methods—including masks and disguises—in the pursuit of justice. I am less interested in superhuman aliens and mutants, although they too can function as vigilantes. And I am not talking at all about superheroes who simply rescue people in peril, which is legal in any system. I am talking about superheroes who take the law into their own hands, who break the law in order to do justice.

Masked vigilantes are staples of literature and legend, including Robin Hood and the Sicilian Vendicatori and Beati Paoli, all from the Middle Ages. But the most well-attested historical examples of masked vigilantes are, of course, the Ku Klux Klan.

Batman breaks the law in order to save the law, when the legal system encounters an opponent that it cannot master. There is a moving scene in Christopher Nolan's *The Dark Knight Rises* in which Commissioner Gordon explains why he turned to Batman, a vigilante, for help:

> There's a point, far out there, when all the structures fail you, and the rules aren't weapons anymore, they're . . . shackles, letting the bad guy get ahead. One day . . . you may face such a moment of

crisis. And in that moment, I hope you have a friend like I did, to plunge their hands into the filth so that you can keep yours clean!

This is a perfect description of the function of the sovereign as described by Schmitt. Sovereignty means supreme political authority within a territory, as opposed to political subjection. Within a society, the sovereign is the ruler, as opposed to the ruled. A sovereign nation rules itself, as opposed to being ruled by others. But what is the essential characteristic of the sovereign? In *Political Theology*, his short book on the concept of sovereignty, Schmitt states that: "Sovereign is he who decides on the exception."[3]

To understand what is exceptional, one needs to understand what is normal. In human affairs, the normal is what usually happens. Normal circumstances can, therefore, be anticipated by legislators, and the laws they create can be enforced by functionaries—police, bureaucrats, judges, etc.—in a simple "deductive" way. If a particular event falls under a general law, justice requires a certain prescribed course of action.

But as Aristotle pointed out, in human affairs, generalizations pertain "not always but for the most part," meaning that there are not just normal circumstances but also exceptional ones. But exceptional circumstances—if they really are exceptional—cannot be anticipated by legislators. Thus merely applying the existing laws in exceptional circumstances cannot produce just results.

Justice, therefore, requires not just following rules in normal circumstances but also exercising discretion in exceptional ones. This act of discretion has two aspects:

---

[3] Carl Schmitt, *Political Theology: Four Chapters on the Concept of Sovereignty*, trans. George Schwab (Cambridge, Mass.: MIT Press, 1988), p. 5.

discerning *that* we are facing an exception and discerning *what* we must do to cope with it.[4]

Such discretion can exist on all levels of the legal system. Cops on the beat, judges in courthouses, and bureaucrats in offices all must discern the just path in exceptional circumstances. Of course the discretion of ordinary policemen, judges, and bureaucrats can be reviewed and overruled by higher-ups in the hierarchy.

But you can't appeal and second-guess forever. Eventually, you will come to a final arbiter, the final decider. The same is true of legislative or judicial deliberation. At some point deliberation has to end. Matters must be decided. Questions must be closed so that we can act.

The supreme law in any system is the constitution. And when the constitution encounters an exceptional situation, there must be a supreme decider: he who decides *that* society is facing an exception, and he who decides *what* to do about the exception. This is the sovereign as Schmitt defines him. He is the supreme power, uniting judicial, legislative, and executive functions.

---

[4] I argue that this discretion presupposes a *prior, intuitive* knowledge of justice, of the right thing to do. We cannot conclude that following a given law produces an unjust outcome in exceptional circumstances unless we have *another* access to justice besides the law itself. Since this knowledge is not articulated in rules, I call it an *intuitive* awareness of justice. This intuitive knowledge has to exist *prior* to our attempts to articulate what justice is. Only because we *already* intuitively know what justice is can we judge general laws to be inadequate to exceptional circumstances. This same intuitive sense of justice also allows us to discern the just course in unique circumstances. Intuition furnishes a non-universal "law" to guide us. Plato's arguments about justice in the *Republic* all depend on this prior, intuitive knowledge of what justice is. In the *Nicomachean Ethics*, Aristotle called this intuitive grasp of justice "equity" (*epieikeia*).

Now a vigilante or superhero does not literally become a sovereign—unless, of course, he pulls off a *coup d'état*. But he performs the *function* of the sovereign by deciding that he faces an exceptional situation and what he must do to fix it. Beyond that, he takes full responsibility for his acts, since all he can appeal to is his own judgment of right and wrong. But unlike a true sovereign, who is honored for serving the common good, the vigilante knows he will be punished. But he is willing to bear the sacrifice.

Many societies make provisions to give individuals plenary powers in emergency circumstances. For instance, in normal circumstances, the Romans like the Spartans divided the executive power. The Spartans had two kings, and the Romans had two consuls, each consul being accompanied by twelve lictors carrying the fasces, the emblems of political authority.

However, in emergency situations, the Romans would appoint a dictator, who was accompanied by 24 lictors, symbolizing the unification of executive power. Emergency situations included fighting wars and quelling insurrections, as well as presiding over religious rituals and civic elections. When necessary, Roman dictators could ignore or break the normal law with impunity. But dictators were appointed only for the duration of the special situation or for a fixed period, after which they surrendered their powers.

Another example of a provision for emergency plenary powers is Article 48 of the Weimar German constitution, which allowed the chancellor to assume dictatorial powers in an emergency. Adolf Hitler appealed to Article 48 to assume dictatorial powers after the Reichstag arson. Those who defend the thesis that "Hitler did nothing wrong" will be pleased to learn that he became dictator in a completely legal manner.

In Christopher Nolan's *The Dark Knight*, prosecutor

Harvey Dent defends Batman's vigilantism by likening it to the role of the Roman dictator: "When their enemies were at the gates, the Romans would suspend democracy and appoint one man to protect the city. It wasn't considered an honor; it was considered a public service." Of course there is an important difference: The Roman dictator was a legal office, whereas Batman is an outlaw. Nevertheless, Bruce Wayne sees Dent as someone who might make Batman unnecessary by performing his functions *within* the legal system.

But that is not really possible, for Gotham is a liberal democracy. One of the basic principles of liberal democracy is "government by laws, not men." Liberals see human decision ("arbitrariness") as a source of injustice, which must be eliminated from the political system. From Schmitt's point of view, however, one cannot eliminate decision from politics. One's only choice is to own up to it, to take responsibility for decision, and to make sure that the best possible people are empowered to decide—or, like liberals, we can try to evade that responsibility.

The liberal idea of government is a machine that runs by impersonal rules to make sure that everyone is treated justly and fairly, but which is indifferent to the quality of the individuals who compose society and the cultivation of virtue. If decision is inevitable, then we have to find and shape the best possible deciders. But if society can simply operate like a machine, human vice and mediocrity are no impediments to good government.

Liberals also believe that if they just put the right procedural rules in place, they do not need to worry about the consequences of acting according to those rules. Thus they are dismissive of political philosophies that depend upon any vision of the future, any notion of a common good or ideal society that we should strive for. You can argue all you like that liberal principles lead to catastrophic consequences—for instance, free trade undermines national sovereignty and First World living standards; the free movement of peoples leads to social alienation, miscegenation, and conflict; or expressive individualism leads to cultural degeneracy, collapsing families, and personal unhappiness—but liberals simply deny that consequences have any moral weight. Instead, they will cling to their procedural notions of the good—their sacred "principles"—even though the world might perish.

Liberalism seeks to evade decision in all aspects of politics. But the fundamental pathology of liberalism is the evasion of specifically *sovereign* decision, which forces the sovereign to function outside the law. Those who would save liberalism from itself, when it fails to meet the challenge of the exception, must sacrifice themselves by becoming outlaws. In Commissioner Gordon's terms, they must "plunge their hands into the filth" of illegality so that public officials like him can keep their hands "clean." Clean according to the laws that are "shackles" rather than "tools" of justice. Clean of "arbitrariness," clean of the responsibility of deciding, clean of sovereignty.

Schmitt teaches us that sovereignty ultimately reposes in men, not laws. This is true even in liberal systems, which refuse to admit it openly. Which just means that liberal democracies are ruled by *secret* sovereigns, men who exercise decision as they hide behind the laws and pretend that their hands are tied, that they are just following orders, that their hands and their consciences are clean.

In liberal society, there are two kinds of secret sovereigns. First, there are the founders, the framers of the constitutional order who *decided* what the fundamental laws will be. As I put it elsewhere:

Laws are ultimately created by decisions. Thus those

who believe that decisions must always be governed by laws are simply abandoning their own freedom and responsibility and choosing to be ruled by the free decisions of those who came before them. Just as the deist model of the universe depends upon divine wisdom to frame its laws and set the machine in motion, liberals depend on the human wisdom of the Founders who created the constitution.[5]

This is why Americans revere the Founders and recoil with horror at the thought of another Constitutional Convention. The founders made fundamental decisions so we don't have to, fundamental decisions that we fear to make. The Founders were great men, and we are lesser ones. The Founders, of course, were not the products of the system they created. But we are.

Second, because the founders of a liberal system cannot anticipate every exceptional circumstance, sovereignty must be exercised in the present day as well. And if no legal provisions are made to give plenary powers to a sovereign in a time of crisis, that means that sovereignty must be exercised outside the law.

This leads us to the concept of the "deep state," which, as far as I know, is the only Turkish contribution to political thought. The idea of the deep state (*derin devlet*) is a coinage of Turkish Islamists. It refers to a shadowy network concentrated in the Turkish military and security services which spreads throughout the bureaucracy and judiciary and intersects with organized crime. The deep state works to maintain Turkey as a secular, nationalist society, primarily working against Islamists, Left-wing radicals, and Kurdish separatists, all of whom threaten the Kemalist order. The deep state is behind at least four

---

[5] Greg Johnson, "Schmitt, Sovereignty, and the Deep State," *Counter-Currents*, August 12, 2014.

Turkish military coups. The failure of the July 2016 coup has given Recip Erdogan the pretext for purging the deep state from Turkish institutions. Time will tell if he has succeeded.

The concept of the deep state needs to be distinguished from other extralegal forces that influence political policy. It is easy to confuse the deep state with such notions as an "establishment," a permanent bureaucracy, secret agencies, smoke-filled rooms, lobbies and pressure groups, political "inner parties," NGOs, and even secret initiatic societies, all of which shape political policy and negotiate between interest groups.

These groups are simply part of politics as usual. Thus in Schmittian terms, they have nothing to do with *sovereignty*, which comes to light only when politics as usual breaks down. The deep state is where sovereignty resides if a system fails to legally institutionalize it. The deep state consists of people who have real power within a given system and who work together, killing or dying if necessary, to preserve the system when it enters a crisis. In James Cameron's 1994 movie *True Lies*, Arnold Schwarzenegger works for a secret US government organization called the Omega Sector. It is named "omega" because it is the system's "last line of defense." That is the function of the deep state.

I believe that the American fascination with superheroes, conspiracy theories, and secret societies feeds upon an awareness that liberal democracy punts on the question of sovereignty. We know that our government is riddled with shadowy networks working to advance special interests at the expense of the body politic. And we desperately hope that at least one of these groups might actually be looking out for the system in a time of crisis.

Since White Nationalists wish to create a new political system in North America, and since we are hoping to be helped by crises in the present system, it behooves us to ask who would kill or die to preserve the American system in such a crisis. Is there an American deep state? If so, where does it lie? If not, where might it emerge?

The military is the most likely place where a deep state would emerge, since soldiers take oaths of loyalty more seriously than politicians and are prepared to kill and die for the present system. But a fatal crisis might include catastrophic military failure. It might involve a standoff between the military and other institutions that can only be resolved by outside parties. In such cases, Bonapartism would no longer be an option.

I don't think that the organized Jewish community would function as a deep state in a crisis. As I argue in another essay:

> Organized Jewry is the most powerful force in America today. In terms of politics as usual, Jews get their way in all matters that concern them. But although organized Jewry surely would intersect with an American sovereign deep state, if America faced a severe constitutional crisis, I do not think that Jews would step in to exercise the sovereign decision-making functions necessary to preserve the system. They would surely try to stave off a crisis for as long as possible, to preserve their wealth and power. Then they would try to milk a crisis for all it is worth. But ultimately, I do not think they would risk their own blood and treasure to *preserve* the American system, for the simple reason that the Jews *today* show no sign of caring about America's long-term viability. It's not their country, and they act like it. They are just using it, and using it up. They are not stewarding it for future generations. Therefore, they will not take responsibility for its preservation. In a real crisis, I think their deepest instinct would be simply to decamp

to friendlier climes.[6]

The sovereign combines ultimate power with ultimate responsibility. Like the captain who goes down with his ship, he knows that the price of failure is death. Jews want wealth and power without responsibility. They'll shrug off dishonor rather than suffer death. They're survivors. Thus, in the end, Jews are just toying with and merchandising the idea of superheroes who constitute deep states and play the sovereign role. But that does not stop White Nationalists from taking the idea seriously and planning accordingly.

First, no matter where an American deep state might emerge, the difference between a true White Nationalist and a mere racially-conscious conservative is that we regard the system's ultimate guardians as our worst enemies. Our goal is not to save this system but to create a new one, which makes us revolutionaries, not conservatives.

And that makes us a different kind of outlaw than Batman, who like so many patriotic and public-spirited white people today, accepts the egalitarian-humanist ethos and thus sacrifices himself to preserve a system rigged to destroy him. We want to create a new system, rigged to encourage our survival and flourishing, not our degradation and destruction.

Second, if White Nationalists are serious about creating sovereign white homelands, we need to think of ourselves as a government in exile, as the guiding intelligence and deep state of a stateless people. Just as the British opposition parties maintain shadow cabinets, we must form a shadow government. A League of Shadows, if you like.[7] Every regime is founded by an elite. Every

---

[6] Greg Johnson, "Schmitt, Sovereignty, and the Deep State."
[7] There are many examples of such shadow governments,

regime is governed by an elite. Every regime turns to an elite in a time of crisis. So let us become that elite. In a world without sovereign white homelands, we must create them. In a world without superheroes, we must become them.

Counter-Currents, July 27, 2016

---

but the one that fits best with the theme of superhero as sovereign vigilante is Operation Nemesis, the secret organization of Armenian exiles formed in Boston in 1920 to assassinate the Turkish architects of the Armenian Genocide, which they proceeded to do, almost to a man. See my review of Eric Bogosian's *Operation Nemesis*, *Counter-Currents*, July 31, 2015. See also Jef Costello's "Welcome to the League of Shadows!," *Counter-Currents*, March 30, 2017.

BIRTH OF A NATION:
H. A. COVINGTON'S NORTHWEST QUARTET.*

H. A. Covington
The Hill of the Ravens
Lincoln, Nebr.: 1stBooks Library, 2003

H. A. Covington
A Distant Thunder
Bloomington, Ind.: Authorhouse, 2004

H. A. Covington
A Mighty Fortress
Bloomington, Ind.: Authorhouse, 2005

H. A. Covington
The Brigade
Philadelphia: Xlibris, 2008

Every time a friend adds another weapon to his arsenal, he says, "I hope to *God* I never have to use this." But he keeps buying them, because they may come in handy. I say the same thing every time I pick up a Harold Covington novel. But I keep reading them. Someday, they may come in handy.

The four novels under review, collectively called the Northwest Quartet, tell the story of the creation of a sovereign White Nationalist state, the Northwest American Republic, out of the territory of the United States sometime in the second or third decade of the twenty-first

---

* This review was written before the appearance of the fifth Northwest novel, H. A. Covington, *Freedom's Sons* (Bloomington, Ind.: Authorhouse, 2013).

century—right around the corner, historically speaking. The NAR comprises the present US states of Washington, Oregon, and Idaho, plus parts of Northern California, Montana, and Wyoming. These states secede from the United States through a bitter five-year guerrilla war fought by the Northwest Volunteer Army. The NVA is an armed political party. Its ideology owes much to German National Socialism, but its tactics are modeled on the Irish Republican Army and the mafia, as well as Muslim organizations like Hamas in Palestine, Hezbollah in Lebanon, and the insurgents who have stymied the United States in Iraq and Afghanistan.

These novels are war stories, and frankly that makes me squeamish. I know that war is an integral part of human history; that it decides the destiny of nations, races, and the world; that it forms a large part of the data of world history and the backdrop of world literature; that one cannot write about men without writing eventually about war. I know that war is an occasion for edifying extremes of human greatness and depravity. I know that one can also derive personal inspiration and useful information from war stories. But I just don't find representations of hatred and violence particularly enjoyable. And the better the writer, the more seductive such representations become, resulting in a kind of sadistic pornography of violence.

Covington is a very good writer, and these novels are very entertaining. Yet they are not war porn. Covington shows war as horrible. It is mostly like a camping trip that drags on way too long: boring, sleepless, nerve-wracking, dirty, and grindingly uncomfortable and inconvenient. But occasionally it is livened up by moments of exhilaration and sheer terror. It is just that he thinks the alternative to war is even worse, for peace with the present system means the oppression, degradation, and eventual extinction of our race. Beyond that, these novels are not meant to be mere entertainment. They are meant to be self-fulfilling prophecies. The author wishes to inspire the creation of a real Northwest American Republic, and his novels are filled with a great deal of sound practical advice about how to do it.

These are not just ordinary war novels, moreover. They belong to a new genre: White Nationalist revolutionary fiction, a genre that was pretty much created by William Pierce's *The Turner Diaries*, written under the pen name Andrew MacDonald. Fans of *The Turner Diaries* will find the Northwest Quartet to their liking. Furthermore, Covington's vision of political change is much more practical and detailed than Pierce's, and although Pierce was a graceful, precise, and often powerful writer, he was not a born storyteller, while Covington is.

Covington calls himself a "hack," but this is false modesty. He is a highly talented novelist, capable of creating vivid three-dimensional characters. He is particularly deft at crafting characters from working-class and Southern backgrounds. Covington also spins complex, gripping plots that move toward deeply moving emotional climaxes. These novels are tear-jerkers. But expect to do a lot of laughing as well, because Covington is also a biting satirist with a wicked sense of humor. He is, moreover, a remarkably versatile stylist—Victor Hugo on one page, Quentin Tarantino on another. In *A Distant Thunder*, *A Mighty Fortress*, and *The Brigade*, Covington's tales of sassy, wisecracking teenage terrorists bring to mind Joss Whedon's *Buffy the Vampire Slayer*, with its virtuosic fusion of apocalyptic horror, intense dramatic conflict, and teenage frivolity. This is high praise in my book.

But the Northwest Quartet is not merely a literary achievement, for these are novels of ideas, and they establish Harold Covington as the most significant American National Socialist thinker since George Lincoln Rockwell. Covington diagnoses what is wrong with America and the current racialist movement, proposes a political solution, and lays out a great deal of sound organizational, strategic, and tactical thinking on how to bring it to fruition. And by communicating these ideas in novels, rather than essays or treatises, Covington assures that they reach a broader popular audience at a deeper emotional and motivational level.

AN OVERVIEW OF THE QUARTET

The Hill of the Ravens (330 pp.) is the first novel to be published, but it is the last in terms of the internal chronology of the Quartet. It is set sometime after the middle of the twenty-first century, several decades after the establishment of the NAR—close enough to the war of independence for many of the veterans to still be living, yet far enough along in the history of the NAR for the regime to have taken shape and the first generation raised under it to be coming of age. Unlike the rest of the Quartet, *The Hill of the Ravens* is not a war novel *per se*, but a detective novel in which the war of Northwest independence is a constant backdrop. Since the novel is set in the future, there are also trappings of science fiction.

A Distant Thunder (364 pp.) is the second novel to be published. In terms of its internal chronology, the frame is set a little later than *The Hill of the Ravens*. An oral history of Shane Ryan, a very old veteran of the Northwest Volunteer Army, is being recorded for posterity. Shane's recollections, however, focus on the period immediately before the war of independence and the war itself. The setting is western Washington State, south of Seattle. *A Distant Thunder* gets off to a rough start, because the literary conceit of an oral history allows Covington to indulge in stream-of-consciousness rambling, which quickly becomes tiresome. But if you stick it out through the first 50 or so pages, you will be glad, for once this book gets you hooked it is a magnificent read.

A Mighty Fortress (364 pp.) is the third novel in order of publication. In terms of the internal chronology, it falls near the end of the war of independence. It is set in the Seattle area, and a large portion of the book is devoted to the Longview Conference in which the United States and the Northwest Volunteer Army negotiate an end to the war.

The final novel of the Quartet, *The Brigade* (735 pp.), is Covington's finest literary achievement. The plot is gripping, the writing is superb, and the climaxes are shatteringly powerful. It is set in western Oregon, in and around Portland. Its story spans the whole war of independence.

A Mighty Fortress is the first novel of the Quartet that I read, and I lucked out, because I think it is the best place to start. Literarily, it is one of the best written and most moving. In these terms, it is second only to *The Brigade*, which is my favorite. But *The Brigade* is 735 pages long, versus 364 pages for *A Mighty Fortress*, and many potential readers will be intimidated by the page count. So begin with *A Mighty Fortress*, get hooked, then read *The Brigade*, followed by *A Distant Thunder*, and finally *The Hill of the Ravens*.

CONDITIONS OF SECESSION

White Nationalists agree on the desirability of a white homeland in North America. The question is how to achieve it. Why is the secession of a White Nationalist republic from the United States a better aim than a completely White Nationalist United States? Why should we be satisfied with a part rather than the whole? Secession is preferable because there simply are not enough of us, and too many of them, for us to save the whole country. We cannot hope to defeat the entire US government and 100 million non-whites. But it is more realistic to hope that a predominantly white area of the country could secede. Secession would not require the destruction of the US government, but only the surrender of some of its territory. (It happened with the Panama Canal Zone, and it could happen again.) The secession of a predominantly white area, moreover, would not entail the moral and logistical nightmare of expelling millions of non-whites.

The strategy of the NVA is to make a large area of the United States ungovernable. The NVA also attacks the regime in its power centers: New York, Washington, D.C., and Hollywood. At a certain point, the regime decides to cut its losses and pull out. As Covington frequently reminds us, in such campaigns it is the accountants who surrender, not the generals. Such wars are difficult undertakings, but they are far easier than full-fledged revolutions. A regime will fight harder for its very existence than for some territory, especially territory remote from the centers of power.

Covington's choice of the Pacific Northwest is logical because it is one of the whitest parts of the country. The Northwest is relatively far from the power centers in New York and Washington, D.C. It is not surrounded by the rest of the United States but has a long Pacific coastline and borders on Canada and (in Covington's scenario) Aztlan. The region is also large and resource-rich enough to aspire to relative economic self-sufficiency, a necessity for a state that would likely face the same sort of political and economic sanctions as Rhodesia and South Africa before they fell to black rule.

Of course no movement as small and sorry as today's White Nationalism is going to wrest one square inch from the US government. Thus the movement must change as well. The first indispensable condition for creating a Northwest American Republic is the concentration of racially-conscious whites in the Pacific Northwest. This will make possible a second condition, namely the creation of a real, face-to-face white racialist community and movement, rather than a merely virtual movement. As

Covington is fond of saying, no revolution will be made by people who are not within driving distance of one another.

Covington believes that such a racially-conscious community must be organized along Communist lines as a revolutionary Party of Northwest independence. The Party has three functions: education (propaganda), recruitment, and preparation. Initially, the Party will operate above ground, carrying out open as well as underground propaganda and recruitment. Covington is scornful of White Nationalist organizations that allow someone to join simply by mailing in a check. The revolution will not have a post office box. It will not take credit cards. It will not be tax-deductible. As Covington likes to say, "You do not join the Party. The Party joins you." It identifies potential members, then carefully investigates and tests them. This keeps out informers and kooks. All recruits will be evaluated as potential political *soldiers*. For, from the moment the Party emerges into the public eye, it is preparing for the day that it is banned. Then it will transform itself into an underground guerrilla army. And while underground, it will be preparing to re-emerge as the government and army of a new society.

Beyond that, no white homeland will emerge unless there are certain moral transformations: Whites as a whole must recover their courage, and movement people need to become much more *serious*. In the novels, Covington speaks of 50,000 racially-conscious whites migrating to the Pacific Northwest in the years before the war of independence. But why the migrants begin to come, why whites recover their courage, and why the movement becomes more serious is described as a complete *mystery*. It would be less of a mystery if these novels became widely read.

But even if the White Nationalist movement became dramatically larger, better-organized, and more serious, it would still be no match for the United States at full strength. Thus the regime must suffer a crisis, or a convergence of crises, before part of the US could hope to secede. The Irish Republic probably would not have gained its independence had the British Empire not been weakened by World War I. India would not have gained its independence had the Empire not been bled dry by World War II.

Fortunately, we know that the US system is moving full steam toward catastrophes on a number of different tracks. The political system is captive to minority and foreign interests and cannot pursue the common good. Our Israel-first foreign adventurism and profligate welfare spending are economically unsustainable. Multiculturalism and non-white immigration are leading to the ever-intensified degradation and dispossession of whites, which can only lead to increased ethnic conflict. Affirmative action and corruption have filled the government with incompetent employees who are parasites at best and actively throttle productivity and sow social chaos at worst. Education and popular culture continue their descent. The system is dependent on ever-increasing technological sophistication to exploit diminishing natural resources, yet the demographic trends are profoundly dysgenic. Morons are reproducing faster than geniuses, and the political system enfranchises and caters to the morons, with their high time preferences and ignorance of the causes of order and wealth. Furthermore, as Sam Dickson has pointed out, the system apparently has no brakes. For example, even before Social Security was enacted, it was known to be unsustainable, but nothing has been done to solve the problem, only to postpone the final crash by a few election cycles. Of course the system might be able to survive one crisis at a time. But eventually several crises will converge, and the United States will not be able to survive intact.

In a mild crisis, the first impulse is to hold on to everything. In a severe crisis, or a convergence of crises, one is forced to choose to surrender some assets to save the rest. Covington's hope is to create a White Nationalist movement that is sufficiently strong to carve off a chunk of the United States when that moment arrives. In Covington's scenario, the US leadership is more concerned about the territorial integrity of Israel than of the United States. This is a reasonable premise, since even today the United States cannot summon the effort and funds to secure its border with Mexico, but it can summon immensely more money and enthusiasm to fight wars in Iraq and Afghanistan at the behest of Israel. (In Covington's scenario, the US is bogged down fighting and occupying practically every Muslim country in the Middle East at Israel's behest, but that is still not enough to stave off Israel's eventual disappearance beneath the Muslim world's rising demographic tide.) Thus, if the regime is forced to choose between supporting Israel and keeping the Pacific Northwest, the Northwest will be allowed to secede.

In Covington's scenario, another factor conducive to the secession of the Pacific Northwest is the regime's decision to acquiesce to the *de facto* Mexican re-conquest of California and the Southwest and allow the creation of Aztlan. As a general rule, it seems prudent for white secessionists to uphold the principle of secession for all peoples, including Mexicans and Hawaiians. However, our rulers have never been too concerned with abstract principles and general rules. But they are clearly wedded to the destruction of the white race. The secession of Aztlan forwards that goal. The secession of the Pacific Northwest does not. Furthermore, the secession of Aztlan might actually increase the regime's ability to hold onto the Pacific Northwest by allowing it to reassign troops and resources to the Northwest.

Other factors that conspire to lay the conditions of

secession include: (1) an ever-increasing population of dispossessed whites who no longer have anything to lose in taking up arms against the regime, (2) large numbers of well-trained and deeply embittered white veterans from the regime's imperial wars, (3) a sufficiently corrupt and incompetent federal government staffed by lunatic ideologues, soulless clock-punchers, and affirmative action drones, and (4) a long process of overt and covert propaganda by the Party designed to increase popular discontent and tensions within the system.

Once these conditions exist, it takes only a galvanizing event, a spark to ignite the conflagration. In Covington's scenario, it is the Coeur d'Alene Uprising, which is modeled on Ireland's Easter Rebellion. The professional meddlers of "It Takes a Village," the federal equivalent of the Department of Family Services, decide to seize the children of a family of apolitical neo-pagans, the Singers, and adopt them out to more suitable parents, who will not read them hateful, racist Norse myths at bedtime. When they resist, they are massacred by federal forces, just like at Waco and Ruby Ridge. But this time, ordinary white people—the Singers' neighbors—spontaneously take up arms against the feds.

Although the Party played no direct role in the initial resistance, it was prepared to seize the opportunity. Party activists—men and women alike—grabbed their guns and rushed to Coeur d'Alene. They declared themselves the Northwest Volunteer Army, hoisted a tricolor flag, and announced the birth of the Northwest Republic. Federal troops were rushed in, and after 16 days and a great deal of bloodshed, the tricolor was hauled down again. But the rebellion was not extinguished and eventually grew into a war of national liberation.

CONDITIONS OF SUCCESS

The Northwest Quartet contains a wealth of practical

ideas that deserve serious consideration.

(1) Loose, Flexible, and Resilient Organizational Structures. Despite the influence of German National Socialism on Covington's thinking, the NVA is not a centralized organization run on the *Führer* principle. Covington is above all a pragmatist, and such an organization would be too vulnerable to destruction by decapitation. Therefore, a loose and resilient organizational model is adopted from the IRA and the Cosa Nostra. The basic unit of the NVA is a three-man cell capable of operating semi-autonomously. Cell-members have only limited knowledge of other cells and the command hierarchy, so that if a cell is infiltrated or a cell member is captured, the potential damage is limited. Cells are parts of brigades, each of which has a commander and a political officer who serves as liaison with the Army Command. The NVA also has "Flying Columns": mobile independent partisan units of 60 to 100 fighters operating in non-urban settings. There are no uniforms, blood oaths, torchlight rituals, and other such trappings, just an atmosphere of ruthless pragmatism and high seriousness in pursuit of victory.

(2) The Paramount Importance of Character. One cannot build an effective revolutionary movement out of defective people. Thus good character is the most important trait the NVA seeks in a member. Character is more important than ideology, skills, social background, financial resources, etc., because without good character, none of these other advantages can be reliably mobilized for the cause. Covington is not just talking about the classical virtues of courage, self-control, and wisdom, but also about traits like maturity and willingness to work with others in the real world, rather than merely in the cyber world of today's movement. Covington is an admirer of Xenophon, who teaches that the army that is strongest in character has the advantage, other things being equal.

(3) The Revolution Must be Dry. Allied with the

character issue is one of Covington's best proposals, General Order 10: For the duration of the struggle, all NVA forces must not use alcohol or drugs. There are three good reasons for this. First, drink and drugs reduce effectiveness and impair judgment, which can lead to disaster. Second, regardless of the consequences, the demand to give up drink and drugs communicates in a very concrete way that this struggle is serious business. By demanding sacrifices from its members, the NVA commands greater respect and dedication. Third, it weeds out unserious people, those who prefer personal indulgence to racial survival.

(4) Religious Neutrality. Covington is adamant that the White Nationalist movement must be neutral on religious questions. The purpose of White Nationalism is to create a white homeland. This is a concrete political goal that people with widely diverging beliefs can pursue for many different reasons. It is more important that we work together for the same goal than have the same reasons for pursuing it. Religion in particular is not a topic that can be discussed rationally, thus nothing good can come from discussing it. Therefore, the topic should be avoided. Furthermore, the movement must take special care not to be, or to appear to be, opposed to the religion of the majority of whites: Christianity.

(5) Fight Smart and Cheap. It is possible for a small guerrilla force to defeat a much larger force by fighting more intelligently. The NVA does not recruit impulsive adrenaline junkies or berserkers with death-wishes. It does not ask people to volunteer for suicide missions and last stands. It does not ask soldiers to die for a white homeland—although they all know the risks. Instead, it asks soldiers to make their enemies die for a white homeland, while preserving their own precious lives to fight another day. The NVA looks for every opportunity to extract large benefits at little or no cost. Phoning in a fake bomb threat costs the NVA nothing, but it costs the enemy dearly in money and manpower. Modern technological society is so complex and interdependent that a small act of sabotage can have enormous and expensive consequences. This is why Covington holds that in such a war, it is not the generals who surrender but the accountants.

(6) Choose One's Targets Carefully. The goal of the NVA is a white homeland. It cannot achieve this by alienating the white populace. Therefore, the NVA chooses its targets carefully and seeks to make the regime's work more difficult while minimizing damage to white civilians. Its chief targets are active functionaries and collaborators of the regime. It also seeks to drive out non-whites by drying up their employment and social support networks. The NVA also seeks to avoid causing death or injury to children of any kind, because this elicits sympathy for non-whites and makes the NVA look like monsters. For the same reasons, the NVA also avoids targeting civilian airliners and religious figures and buildings, no matter how odious.

(7) Deliver Concrete Benefits to Whites. The NVA does not just fight the system. It also seeks to deliver tangible benefits to the white populace. By driving out non-whites, the NVA produces job opportunities and rising wages for whites, lower crime rates, and a visibly more homogeneous community. By targeting the regime's tax collection system, the NVA ensures that white workers have more take-home pay. The goal is to persuade the white populace of the benefits of White Nationalism by actually delivering them during the war itself. This is one way in which the NVA positions itself to emerge at the end of the struggle as the government of a new nation.

(8) Destroy the System's Credibility. While the NVA works to increase its credibility with the populace, it also works to destroy the system's credibility by attacking its buildings, personnel, and allies. If the system can no longer protect itself, the people will conclude that it can no longer protect them as well. Again, the NVA is selective, focusing on federal and state rather than local governments. Wherever possible, the NVA seeks a *modus vivendi* with local law enforcement. If local police look the other way when the NVA is around, the NVA will leave them alone to protect the citizens.

THE REPUBLIC REALIZED

The Hill of the Ravens is Covington's guided tour of the Northwest American Republic several decades after its birth. At the beginning of the novel, the main character, Colonel Donald Redmond of the Bureau of State Security, is called to the office of the President of the Republic, his father-in-law John Corbett Morgan. He is given a secret and highly sensitive mission: to reopen the investigation into the betrayal and massacre of the Olympic Flying Column during the war of independence. Tom Murdock, the commander of the Olympic Flying Column, and his lover Melanie Young are among the greatest heroes of the Republic. Gertrude Greiner, who betrayed them to the US government, is one of its greatest villains. Thus when Trudy Greiner resurfaces after decades of hiding in Aztlan and announces she plans to return to the Republic to clear her name, she threatens to tear a gaping hole in the mythology of the young nation.

Moreover, if she does clear her name, this will necessarily cast the shadow of suspicion on the other eight survivors of the Olympic Flying Column. In the following years, some of these survivors came to number among the Republic's most distinguished citizens: Admiral David Leach, the Chief of Staff of the *Kriegsmarine*; SS Major General William Vitale; Frank Palmieri, the NAR's Minister of Transport; Dr. Joseph Cord, the Republic's most brilliant scientist (clearly a portrait of William Pierce, a man Covington despises); and Dragutin Saltovic, an internationally-renowned classical pianist. If any of these men were traitors, it would be far worse for the Republic than the mere exoneration of Trudy Greiner.

Redmond's investigation provides an ideal framework for a guided tour of the Northwest American Republic—touching on the political system, the military, economics, education, science, culture, and religion—which is Covington's pedagogical purpose. (My only criticism of this book as a novel is that it feels a bit too much like a guided tour.) The NAR is a society of 40 million racially-conscious white people from all over the globe. It borders on Canada to the north, the United States to the east, and Aztlan to the south.

Because it is a relatively small country surrounded by chaotic and hostile neighbors, the NAR is characterized by high levels of military training and preparedness and high levels of spending on defense and research and development, including a space program. The NAR also has a War Prevention Bureau, an organization dedicated to assassinating foreign enemies of the NAR who try to stir up wars against it. If Saddam Hussein had been half the villain he was made out to be, he could have saved countless Iraqi lives—including his own—with such an organization.

The NAR also provides education and health care and guarantees full employment. A ministry of culture ensures that the glories of European high culture are both preserved and accessible to all. In one of Covington's many amusing touches, the ministry also exerts subtle pressures on dress and has apparently managed to turn back the clock to Edwardian or Victorian fashions—let us hope they stop short of powdered wigs, codpieces, and bearskins—giving the novel an archeofuturistic flavor. (One advantage of fascism is that it does give men more opportunities to dress up.) The NAR is also a "green" society, which prioritizes public transportation, non-polluting technologies, nature preservation, and even uses *Jurassic*

Park technologies to bring back extinct species (another wrinkle on archeofuturism).

Although the government of the NAR is strong and centralized—indeed authoritarian—it is no dictatorship. The NAR is a mixed regime with legislative and executive branches—multiple centers of power that check and balance each other in accordance with the Republic's constitution. There is also a popular dimension to government. There is universal suffrage. Since women took up arms to fight for the Republic, they also have the vote. But there are different levels of citizenship, and the higher levels come with more votes, ensuring that quality reigns over mere quantity. Although founded as a one-party state, different "tendencies" have emerged within the Party, effectively splintering it into a multiparty system. All this seems decidedly odd for a movement inspired by German National Socialism. But Covington posits that the NVA could succeed only by rejecting the *Führer* principle and adopting a decentralized, informal cell structure, and the pluralistic regime he describes seems like a natural outgrowth of this organizational strategy.

The NAR, like the racialist movement today, is also divided between different religious camps, chief among them Christianity, Christian Identity, neo-paganism, and complete non-believers, who are always on the verge of strife. Because of this, the NAR ensures freedom of religion and the separation of religion and state. Managing the religious situation requires a delicate balancing act among the leadership. One of Covington's most interesting and wryly ironic ideas is that in such a situation, National Socialism would serve as a force for moderation.

Libertarian-leaning people will rejoice to learn that the government of the NAR, though strong and influential, is also *small*. There are two mains reasons for this. First, when left to their own devices, white people create ordered liberty as surely as blacks create chaos, so there is no need for state control of vast sectors of life. Second, government must be large when it goes against the grain of nature, specifically when it tries to make unequal individuals and races equal. When we abandon the lies of equality and multiracialism and let nature take its course, government does not need to be very big. Taxes are low and money is sound. There is so much privacy and freedom of movement that the secret police (a very small agency, directed mostly at external enemies) have trouble even *locating* individuals. (Try losing the government in today's "land of the free.") There is religious freedom and the right to bear arms. Covington evidently dislikes lawyers and envisions a minimal legal system that any citizen can understand.

Far more important, however, is the fact that the Northwest American Republic ensures *positive* liberty for healthy biological and cultural development. The NAR is a society in which men are free to be men; women are free to be women; and children are free to grow up in a healthy and beautiful environment, free of America's chaos and violence, drugs and degeneracy, junk food and junk culture. It is a society in which whites are free to act according to their innate sense of decency; to create according to their innate sense of beauty; to apply their genius to discovering the secrets of nature and solving the problems of living; to give free reign to their questing and adventurous spirit.

The worst aspects of Covington's vision are his "day of the rope" revenge fantasies, which smack more of Old Testament superstition and self-righteousness than of Aryan reason. These can only repulse otherwise sympathetic readers and make our enemies' work easier. The NAR is no utopia, then. But even with its imperfections, Covington has given us a vision—maybe even a world-transforming myth—that deserves to be taken seriously.

I highly recommend the Northwest Quartet. Besides

being enjoyable and informative, these novels deliver another important benefit. White Nationalism is almost entirely a virtual movement of geographically scattered individuals connected by the internet and print publications. There is very little face-to-face community and real-world activism. Because of this, the movement has an overall tone of self-indulgence and frivolity. Whether or not one ultimately accepts Covington's outlook, nobody can read these books without coming away with a much more *serious* attitude about White Nationalism and the conviction that we need real community, real activity, real dedication, and self-sacrifice. Perhaps the best compliment I can pay these books is that they are so subversive that someday the government will have to ban them. So get your copies today.

The Occidental Quarterly, vol. 9, no. 1, Spring 2009

Farnham O'Reilly's *Hyperborean Home*

Farnham O'Reilly
Hyperborean Home
Xlibris, 2011

Hyperborean Home pioneers a new and absolutely necessary genre: racial nationalist fantasy literature, specifically Traditionalist, deep ecological, esoteric "Nature's Witnessist," "Natural Selectionist" fantasy literature. (We will get to those terms later.) Its only real precursor might be some of the novels of Ernst Jünger, such as *Visit to Godenholm*,[1] but even that is a stretch.

One of the common themes of many Counter-Currents writers is the insufficiency of backwards-looking conservatism and data-driven empiricism to preserve and elevate our race. History and natural science are, of course, necessary for understanding the world. But we want to do more than understand the world. We want to change it. We want to create a future for our people. And for that, facts are not enough.

Facts appeal only to a small number of intellectually inclined people. Furthermore, on their own, the facts about our present circumstances are more likely to produce despair than action. What we need is a myth, meaning a concrete vision, a story of who we are and who we wish to become.[2] Since myths are stories, they can be understood and appreciated by virtually anyone. And myths,

---

[1] Ernst Jünger, *Visit to Godenholm*, trans. Annabel Moynihan (Stockholm: Edda Publishing, 2015).

[2] See Michael O'Meara, "The Myth of Our Rebirth," *Counter-Currents*, September 10, 2010.

unlike science and policy studies, resonate deeply in the soul and reach the wellsprings of action. Myths can inspire collective action to change the world.

I will not soon be forgiven for claiming that a group of Tolkien fanatics who decide to breed a super-race of elves has a greater chance of preserving the white race than the current White Nationalist movement with its mighty arsenal of bell curves, pie charts, darky stories, and nostalgic pining for Jim Crow, the Third Reich, the Confederacy, or still more distant times.[3] I think I have found a kindred spirit in Farnham O'Reilly.

Hyperborean Home is set on earth 3,000 years in the future. The human population has been dramatically reduced. Those who remain live simple lives in harmony with Mother Nature. In the northern parts of North America, Europe, and Australia—and probably other areas, like southern South America and New Zealand—dwell the Fairest Ones. Other races dwell in other parts of the world: Orientals, Blacks, Amerindians, Middle Eastern Muslims, etc.

The different races occupy separate, homogeneous homelands. All races are concerned with preserving their genetic distinctness. The main cause of racial hatred—different races being forced together in the same living space—has been eliminated. The global capitalist system seems also to have been eliminated. Thus race relations are harmonious. For the most part, the races seem to have no contact with one another. But on the highest levels, there are cordial friendships between leaders that allow them to unite and fight for their common survival when an ancient evil returns.

Science Fiction is supposedly oriented toward a tech-

---

[3] See my essay, "Is Racial Purism Decadent?" in *Confessions of a Reluctant Hater*, second edition (San Francisco: Counter-Currents, 2016).

nological future, fantasy to an archaic past. But just as *Star Wars* is set "A long time ago, in a galaxy far, far away," there is nothing to prevent us from locating a fantasy novel in the future. Indeed, if one goes far enough into the future, highly-evolved beings might appear to us as archaic and even primitive in their ways of life, and highly-evolved technology might seem like magic.

So the boundaries of science fiction and fantasy are fluid. Indeed, some of the best science fiction is archeofuturist: combining high technology with archaic values and social forms. The paradigm of archeofuturist fiction is Frank Herbert's *Dune*.

Hyperborean Home is also archeofuturistic. The Fairest Ones can live without a lot of modern technology because they have focused on selective breeding—eugenics, combined with euthanasia for the culls—to improve the human body. The Fairest Ones, like Tolkien's elves, live enormously long lives. They are extraordinary strong and beautiful. They are resistant to disease and even to radiation. They can communicate telepathically with one another and with animals. (Domestic animals have also been dramatically bred up over 3,000 years.)

Because of their biological improvements, the fairest ones can live without a lot of technology that we take for granted. But we also learn that they still prize scientific research as well as technological development to do things they still cannot do unaided. For one thing, the Fairest Ones are dedicated to erasing all traces of the technological Old Order and restoring all the things it destroyed, including countless species of animals and plants, which have been brought back with *Jurassic Park* technologies. The Fairest Ones also have flying machines for rapid transportation. They also did a great deal of research into space travel. But the most advanced among them are now beginning to experiment with teleportation, which will render even this technology irrelevant.

The Fairest Ones are ruled by Seers, 88 men and women of advanced age, refined wisdom, and unusual powers. They are basically wizards. Their policies are executed by a martial-religious order called the Seer Service—the SS for short.

The Fairest Ones live in extended families, and their dogs are integral parts of their families and inseparable companions. They live in agrarian communities. There are few cities, and they are small. They value education. They are vegetarians and apparently do not drink or smoke. They are monogamous and prize sexual modesty and discretion.

The Fairest Ones are intensely religious. They worship the Allfather and Mother Nature. They believe that from time to time, the divine takes on human form—an avatar—and enters into the world to set things right. They believe that at least some souls reincarnate. They believe that they descended from a race that spread across the world from a Hyperborean Homeland, settling for a while in a place called Atlantis.

What is the philosophy of the Fairest Ones? What led their distant ancestors to steer their posterity in such a direction, to create such a world? The Fairest Ones are followers of a figure known only as Nature's Witness. According to the teaching of a figure known as the First Priestess, Nature's Witness was a divine avatar who entered the world to do battle with the Old Order, also known as Six Sixty-Six, and create a New Order in which mankind lives in harmony with nature. The philosophy of Nature's Witness is called Natural Selectionism—NS for short. I am pretty sure that Nature's Witness is Adolf Hitler, and the First Priestess is Savitri Devi.

The principal enemies of Natural Selectionism are known as the Evil Ones and "Urban Men." The Evil Ones believe that man is not part of nature. They also believe that they are the only real men. All the other two-legged mammals are mere beasts of burden. They believe that their God, who is also not part of nature, gave them dominion over nature and other men. Accordingly, they instituted a way of life involving the exploitation of nature and other men, including the promotion of race-mixing, by which they hoped to render their two-legged beasts of burden docile and incapable of resisting them. The Evil Ones sound suspiciously like the Jews.

The Evil Ones based their religion on something known as the Black Book, which sounds like the Bible. Later, an avatar appeared among them, the One Who Came Before. He tried to civilize them, but they killed him. This sounds like Jesus. Then an Evil One known as the Great Deceiver twisted his teachings into an instrument by which the Evil Ones spiritually poisoned and enslaved the rest of mankind. That would be Saint Paul as depicted by Savitri Devi. The Evil Ones, however, apparently did not survive the fall of the Old Order. And the religion of the Great Deceiver has apparently died out among the Fairest Ones, replaced completely by Natural Selectionism.

The Evil Ones also martyred Nature's Witness—driving him to suicide, just like Hitler—but his spirit rose from his grave, and with the help of the First Priestess, the First Disciple (who was also martyred—my guess would be George Lincoln Rockwell), and others, Natural Selectionism became a militant faith against time which eventually, by any means necessary, brought about the downfall of the Old Order before the Evil Ones could consummate their plan to completely destroy the Fairest Ones.

I will say little more about the plot of *Hyperborean Home* than can be gathered from the book jacket: an ancient evil has apparently reawakened, threatening the survival of the world. Thus the Fairest Ones and all the other races of the earth, as well as members of the animal kingdom—including some giant creatures previously thought to be mythical—must join together to defeat evil forever.

Come to think of it, that is pretty much the story of *The Lord of the Rings*, without necessarily being derivative of it. (At this level of generality, there are not that many stories anyway.) Trust me, if you love Tolkien, you will find it hard to resist this book.

Hyperborean Home is a remarkable achievement. It is imaginative and beautifully-written, with a captivating narrative. The book is also attractively designed and well-edited, and I am very picky about such things.

It is not, however, without flaws.

First, the didactic elements could be better integrated into the story. The lessons on the nature of the Old Order run on a little long, and pedagogically, they begin with a very odd topic: accounting practices! A far more dramatic and logical starting point would have been the lessons on the Black Book of the Evil Ones, which is ushered into the classroom with an SS guard and only touched with gloves, its pages turned with wooden paddles. Surely the accounting lessons could have been put in an appendix. (The novel itself is 317 pages, with 70 pages of appendices at the back—not unlike Tolkien either.)

Second, there is a stylistic imbalance. The early chapters, which I find quite captivating, have a leisurely pace and are filled with detailed descriptions. It often reminds me of Ernst Jünger at his best. (But, unfortunately, even at his best Jünger can be somewhat boring.) The middle chapters get bogged down in didactic lessons. The last chapters have a much faster-paced narrative, but the style becomes less like nuanced fantasy literature, more like pulp adventure fiction. A better model for such blow-by-blow writing would be the *Iliad* (the father of all sportscasting, among other things).

Finally, the Fairest Ones' attitudes about sexuality, including their exaggerated horror of homosexuality, have much more to do with the Black Book of the Evil Ones than with our own authentic history and culture.

But these are minor quibbles when compared to the virtues of this remarkable book. One must also take into account that this is apparently the author's first novel. I hope it is the first of many: not just other novels by Farnham O'Reilly, but of a whole new genre and literary school.

I wish that Counter-Currents had published this book, and as a publisher, that is one of the nicest things I can say about it.

Counter-Currents, July 8, 2011

NOTES ON CHUCK PALAHNIUK'S *ADJUSTMENT DAY*

Chuck Palahniuk's *Adjustment Day*[1] is a highly imaginative and entertaining novel that reflects a long and deep immersion in the online world of White Nationalism, from the best of it to the worst and all shades in between.

I don't have much to add to the reviews of *Adjustment Day* by Jef Costello and James O'Meara,[2] so I wish to focus here on some of Palahniuk's thoughts about how an ethnonationalist revolution might occur, and how it might go wrong.

1. CAN AN ETHNONATIONALIST REVOLUTION BE MADE BY A MULTI-RACIAL COALITION?

In *Adjustment Day*, the ethnonationalist revolution is created by a coalition of "ethnic" groups—whites, blacks, and gays—that wish to create separate homelands for themselves after the revolution and then go their separate ways. Jews, Asians, race-mixers, and mestizos don't take part in the revolution and have no ethnostate in the end. Instead, they are forced to flee.

It is a perennial debate in White Nationalist circles whether we should seek alliances with non-white ethnonationalist groups. The trouble with these discussions

---

[1] Chuck Palahniuk, *Adjustment Day: A Novel* (New York: W. W. Norton & Co., 2018).

[2] Jef Costello, "A Gift Greater than *Fight Club*?: Chuck Palahniuk's *Adjustment Day*," *Counter-Currents*, August 31, 2018, and James J. O'Meara, "'Most Likely You Go Your Way and I'll Go Mine': Stephen King's *Fight Club*," *Counter-Currents*, September 7, 2018.

is that they ignore the nature of alliances, which are generally *temporary* and *made possible by emergencies*, i.e., interruptions in the normal order of things. If circumstances arose in which White Nationalists and, say, the Nation of Islam have common concrete interests and can ally to achieve them, I have little doubt that such an alliance could take place. The same is true of any other non-white ethnic group, including Jews. But once the specific circumstances of the alliance have passed, the two groups would go back to normal, i.e., they would return to distrusting and despising one another.

2. The Revolution Could Not Have Happened without Elite Sponsorship.

Walter Baines is a pathetic white drug addict who decides to start his life over by kidnapping an oligarch and forcing him to be his "new old man"— i.e., a mentor and father figure. So he drives to New York City and kidnaps Talbott Reynolds.

Reynolds tells Walter that he has a hidden transmitter beneath his skin, which precipitates a long and gruesome scene in which the junkie practically flays Talbott alive. Such an ordeal would cause the strongest of minds to break. It causes Talbott to create a revolution. Duck-taped to a chair and covered with blood, Talbott dictates the handbook of the revolution, *Adjustment Day*, to Walter and instructs him on how to publish it, disseminate it, and gather together the leaders of the revolution.

But the revolution needs a crisis to coalesce around, so Talbott calls Senator Holbrook Daniels and orders him to create the National War Resolution, which will start a war in the Middle East to cull millions of restive Millennial males, giving these men a reason to put down their game sticks and pick up rifles. Obviously, Talbott must be a very powerful person to give orders like that. Question: Could Talbott Reynolds be the mysteriously vanished President of the United States?

3. **NO REVOLUTIONARY DOCTRINE OR PRACTICE IS BETTER THAN THE WEAKEST VESSEL BY WHICH IT IS TRANSMITTED.**
The fact that Walter Baines, the midwife of the revolution, is a drug-addled loser with an over-heated fantasy life means that he is not a reliable scribe or organizer. For instance, we learn that the title of Talbott's book is supposed to be *A Judgment Day*, but Walter mis-heard it. One wonders how many other mistakes the book contains. Could these mistakes be the cause of the absurd idea of a gay "ethnostate" or the dystopian elements of Caucasia, the white ethnostate?

4. **SHARIA IS NOT WHITE.**
Palahniuk's vision of Caucasia is presented as a satire of White Nationalism to get it past Leftist gatekeepers in publishing and the media. But it is really just a satire of a particular type of White Nationalism, namely the *unnuanced* anti-intellectual, anti-cultural, anti-urban, anti-woman, anti-gay, anti-egalitarian tendency that basically reduces White Nationalism to raising white birthrates and the Renaissance-Fair LARPing that arises from fetishizing "Tradition" (as if all traditions are good fits for white people) and "hierarchy" (as if all hierarchies are just). Pretty much all these tendencies cluster around the "White Sharia" meme, so that is how I will designate it.

Talbott's case for ethnonationalism is based on the desire for community. But the form of society he creates is essentially anti-communitarian and feudal, because money is created and distributed through the "lineages" of the revolutionary organizers, who form a new aristocracy, while the rest of the population is reduced to peons begging for work on plantations. To survive, people must flatter the new lords into giving them livings. Agriculture and birthing babies become the focus of society. Science, technology, and culture are deemphasized. Objective merit and expertise are deemphasized, replaced by quacks who are practiced at flattering powerful morons. Polygamy arises, which raises the question: What happens to community among men when some have hundreds of wives and hundreds have none? (Perhaps these single men will need to be culled in a war.)

Although Caucasia is decked out in Medieval European garb, the presence of polygamy and the absence of a non-reproductive culture-creating priestly caste actually makes it closer to Islam, hence "White Sharia." But Islam is not a good fit for white people. It is a profoundly backward and inferior civilization that suffocates the human spirit. Although it is unmatched in its ability to pump out inbred orclets. In *Adjustment Day*, Caucasia is inferior even to Blacktopia. Question: How can a white ethnostate survive in a hostile world if it turns its back on science and technology?

If white community really is important, then certain egalitarian-populist measures are called for. First, marriage should be monogamous. Second, the freedom of all citizens to speak their own minds and pursue their own destinies should be safeguarded by the broad distribution of private property. Third, instead of letting jumped-up potentates spend newly-created money first, which warps all of society around them, if every adult citizen received a universal basic income,[3] there would be much greater freedom. (Furthermore, broadly distributed freedom from scarcity would create the conditions for the flourishing of science, technology, and the arts.) Fourth, the gross excesses of the powerful could be curbed or eliminated by giving the populace some sort of political power.

---

[3] On universal basic income, see my essay on Social Credit economics, "Money for Nothing," in *Truth, Justice, & a Nice White Country* (San Francisco: Counter-Currents, 2016).

In short, virtually all of the dystopian elements of Caucasia could be eliminated simply by replacing its feudal model of government with a classical republican model, which treats widely distributed private property and the enfranchisement of the people as a bulwark against tyranny. What could be more "trad" than Aristotle's *Politics*?[4]

Counter-Currents, January 30, 2024

---

[4] See my essay "Introduction to Aristotle's *Politics*," in *From Plato to Postmodernism* (San Francisco: Counter-Currents, 2019).

AYN RAND'S *IDEAL:* THE NOVEL & THE PLAY

Ayn Rand
Ideal: The Novel and the Play
New York: New American Library, 2015

Ideal is Ayn Rand's "lost" second novel, now found and published.

In 1934, after the completion of her first novel, *We the Living*, Ayn Rand wrote a short novel called *Ideal*. At 32,000 words, it is 50% longer than *Anthem*, Rand's third novel (or novella). Dissatisfied, Rand left the novel *Ideal* in relatively unpolished form, then recast it as a relatively polished stage play, which she nevertheless did not see fit to publish.

The play of *Ideal* was published in 1984, two years after Rand's death, in *The Early Ayn Rand: A Selection from Her Unpublished Fiction*, ed. Leonard Peikoff (New York: New American Library, 1984). It was also reprinted in 2005 in *Ayn Rand, Three Plays*, ed. Richard Ralston (New York: New American Library, 2005).

The novel of *Ideal*, however, was set aside and basically forgotten until 2012, when Rand scholar Richard Ralston decided to give it a closer look. It has now been published alongside the play in a handsome volume of 246 pages.

It is easy to see why Ayn Rand never saw fit to publish either version of *Ideal*, for it is not very good.

Her main reservation, probably, is that the plot lacks dramatic necessity. Both novel and play consist of a prologue, six scenes, and an epilogue. The main scenes are encounters between the heroine, movie goddess Kay Gonda, and six of her fans. Save for the last one, these vignettes could be presented in any order merely by changing details about the time of day. Rand, however, believed that good plots had greater dramatic necessity, so no two episodes could simply switch places. Of course, most novels—including many great ones—lack such tight plots, so *Ideal* fails as a story only because of Rand's particular standards. In truth, the story is captivating enough to grab and maintain anyone's interest.

To my mind, the real failures of *Ideal* are that the story rests upon an absurd premise and features a repulsively twisted heroine (and hero), although I fear that Rand did not see things this way. Since the story has been published for three decades now, I have no compunction about summarizing the whole thing.

The heroine of *Ideal* is Kay Gonda, a mysterious Garbo-like screen idol, who is jaded, bored, aloof, and extremely lonely. When an ex-boyfriend Granton Sayres (loosely modeled on J. Paul Getty) commits suicide, Gonda instructs her press agent to spread the rumor that she is a suspect in his murder. Then she takes six particularly overripe and adulatory fan letters from Los Angles-based readers and visits each author to ask for help—and not just help with a flat tire, but help getting away with murder. She wants to see if any of the people who profess to idealize her will actually risk anything for her in real life.

This strikes me as an utterly idiotic premise for a story. An actress spends her entire life, on and off screen, projecting images. Fans consume these images and develop equally imaginary relationships with their creators. Some of them are even moved to share their fantasies in fan letters. It is all good fun. But when you subtract everything specious in your relationship with such people, there is really nothing left. They are just nullities. So if your favorite actress comes to you in the real world and asks you become an accessory after the fact to murder, only a lunatic would grant that request.

Rand, however, thinks this is a hideous betrayal of their "ideals." But Kay Gonda is not an ideal. She is just an image. And when the real thing turns up on your doorstep claiming to be a murderess, the image gets a bit tarnished. So who has really betrayed "Kay Gonda" the image: Kay Gonda or her fans?

Beyond that, being unwilling to overturn one's life to help a wanted criminal based on her screen performances is certainly *not* equivalent to selling out one's honor, one's obligations, and one's moral principles—one's *actual* ideals. What kind of person would be willing to risk ruin over a screen infatuation? And would you really want to meet him? And if Kay Gonda does, what does that say about her psychology?

Gonda's first visit is to George S. Perkins, who after 20 years has just been promoted to Assistant Manager of the Daffodil Canning Company. George is a milquetoast with vaguely romantic aspirations of touring the Alps and watching swans. He has a nagging wife, a nagging mother in law, and three children, ranging from middle school to drooling infancy. In the play, he has two children, but the wife announces she is pregnant with number three. George presses her to have an abortion, because he wants to spend his additional income on a European vacation. (Rand herself apparently terminated at least one pregnancy to pursue her career.) Rand portrays George as a weakling and domestic life as hellishly sordid. She has utter contempt for bourgeois domesticity and breeders.

Then Kay Gonda shows up, representing the embodiment of all of George's painfully inarticulate romantic longings. She asks him for help and tells him flat out that he risks losing his wife, family, and career over it. To Rand and Gonda, of course, these count as nothing. But they mean something to George, so he decides to pass. Rand, of course, treats this as the blackest treason to values, but in truth, George simply realizes that his life and family have greater value than his infatuation with a tarnished movie star.

In the novel, the next person Kay visits is Jeremiah Sliney, an old hick who is facing foreclosure and eviction a few days after his 50th wedding anniversary and can't count on any help from his ungrateful children. When Kay Gonda shows up, Sliney and his wife decide they would rather turn her in for some reward money than spend their last days homeless and hungry. Rand regards them as utterly depraved to pass up an opportunity—at considerable risk to themselves—to aid and abet a glamorous killer before they are deposited into the dustbin. Obviously, their lives are of no worth compared to hers, because it is not everyone who can enthrall millions with languid gestures, doe-eyed yearning, and ecstatic posturing on movie screens.

The portrayal of the Sliney's as sub-literate moronic hicks—Ma and Pa Kettle complete with critters living somewhere in L.A.—is so clumsy that Rand violently struck it out of her typescript. In the play she replaced them with Chuck and Fanny Fink, a couple of Communists who are willing to turn in Kay for the reward money in order to hire a lawyer for Fanny and some of her comrades, who are in legal trouble because of the death of a scab in a violent protest. The satire is still clumsy in places, but overall it is a vast improvement. In both versions, however, I find it hard to fault their decisions. They are not betraying their values but simply subordinating lower values (an infatuation with a tarnished screen idol) to higher values (holding onto one's home or one's freedom). But for Rand, these people's lives should mean less to them than Kay Gonda's.

Next Kay visits Dwight Langley, a handsome, self-absorbed painter on the brink of success. He has just won his first prize and is celebrating. All of his canvases are images of Kay Gonda. When Kay Gonda herself shows up at his apartment, however, he does not even recognize her, then refuses to believe she is Kay Gonda, then angrily orders her out. He does not "betray" his ideal for another value, because he cannot even see that she is there. You see, he is supposed to be a "Platonist," who does not believe that ideals can be real.

As satire, it is shockingly clumsy. First, if he were literally a Platonist, he would not paint either. Second, if he really were a skilled painter who had made a close study of Gonda's appearance, he would have recognized her immediately and would not have any doubts about her identity.

After that, Kay visits the tabernacle of low-church evangelist Claude Ignatius Hix. The episode has some amusing satire of rival evangelist Sister Essie Twomey, but Rand's understanding of American low church Protestants has all the subtlety you would expect from an atheist Russian Jew. For instance, for both Hix and Sliney, statues of the Virgin Mary are meaningful points of comparison.

Hix's creed is more clearly sketched out in the play. It resembles no Protestant theology that I know of so much as the preaching of the con man Onnie Jay Holy in Flannery O'Connor's *Wise Blood* (1952) that there is a "little rosebud of sweetness" in every human soul, i.e., that man is born innocent but corrupted by the world—in short, the Rousseauian notion of the natural goodness of man, which has nothing Christian about it.

Hix thinks Gonda is an embodiment of that ideal on the screen, but when he learns that she is a murderess, he naturally concludes that she needs to repent and pay for her crime—and the publicity of being the guy who persuades her to turn herself in wouldn't hurt Hix either. Again, Rand wants us to think that this is the blackest of betrayals, but this is irrational. Hix actually remains loyal to his values, and he will not betray them to help an actress get away with murder. Beyond that, Hix thinks that getting away with murder would be bad for Gonda's soul, whereas repentance would be good. So he is actually trying to help her, not betray her.

Kay then calls on Dietrich von Esterhazy. The Esterhazys, of course, are a half-step below the Hapsburgs in the Austro-Hungarian aristocracy, but in the play, Rand claims he is from Germany. An exile, playboy, and spendthrift, he is as jaded and world-weary as Gonda herself. On the very evening she arrives, he has just written a bad check. His vast fortune has been spent down to nothing, and he has resolved on suicide. Given that he has nothing to lose and an illustrious lineage of chivalrous forbears, it actually makes sense for him to risk everything to help a damsel in distress. But then all that chivalry crap goes out the window when, overcome by lust and cynicism, he tries to rape her. (In the novel, he actually does.) It is the only scene that is psychologically plausible and that features a genuine betrayal of the character's values.

Finally, Kay visits Johnnie Dawes, the "hero" of the tale, a depressed and alienated loser who decides to redeem his meaningless existence by confessing to a murder that never even happened—and then killing himself.

A man is dead because Kay Gonda pretended to be a murderess to test the devotion of her fans. When Mick Watts, Gonda's drunken Irish Catholic press secretary who is in total thrall to her personality (rather like Rand's drunken Irish Catholic husband Frank O'Connor), angrily confronts her with the enormity of what she has done, Gonda coolly replies, "That was the kindest thing I have ever done." It may be true, but even Stalin could boast of kinder acts.

Kay Gonda wears the triple crown of narcissism, Machiavellianism, and sociopathy. Other people are simply not real to her. Their lives have no meaning beyond what they can do for her. So giving Johnnie Dawes a reason to die for her—even a fraudulent one—is an act of kindness. Like I said, our heroine is twisted and repulsive. But Rand had a thing for sociopaths.

Reading the novel and play versions of *Ideal* side by side is very instructive. One sees how the same story can be told in both genres. Although the play is much more polished than the novel, the novel is still superior in some places.

For instance, the prologue of the play has six characters milling around on stage delivering Kate Hepburn-style rapid-fire dialogue. The effect is exhausting and brings to mind a pen full of yapping dogs. In the novel, an investigative reporter visits one character after another, allowing one to better assimilate the back story and giving a feeling for forward motion rather than frantic milling.

I also found the Esterhazy scene somewhat better fleshed out in the novel. There is some chemistry and cute flirtation between him and Gonda. But we also learn that Esterhazy is a Nietzschean who believes that people are unequal (obviously true), and that superior people should have the right to kill their inferiors, no questions asked (as a fascist, this offends me). But in every other scene, the play is superior.

Of course, there are some points where the novel and play cannot be compared. The novel offers descriptions that the play must leave to the imagination. The novel also gives insights into motivations (particularly Hix's) that can only be inferred in the play.

Rand's writing is uneven in *Ideal*, much more so in the novel than the play. I found myself chuckling at her alienated satire of Hollywood and bourgeois American life ("old ladies whose faces could sweeten the blackest cup of coffee") and cringing at the hazy purple prose of the fan letters, which I hope is satire but fear is not.

Ideal is an entertaining but flawed product of Rand's early Nietzschean-misanthropic phase, before her philosophy or her literary skills had fully matured. So really, there's nothing ideal about it. Although it is easy to see why Rand never published *Ideal*, her legions of readers will be grateful that her heirs did not honor her wishes.

Counter-Currents, November 14, 2024

The Meaning of Mishima's Death

It was fifty years ago today that Yukio Mishima, one of Japan's most celebrated men of letters and an ardent man of the Right, committed suicide at the age of forty-five. What happened, and what did it mean?

On November 25, 1970, Mishima and four followers wearing the uniforms of his private militia group the Shield Society (*Tatenokai*) visited the Ichigaya Barracks of the Japan Self-Defense Force (the *Jieitai*). They took Commander Kanetoshi Mashita hostage then demanded that the troops be assembled so Mishima could address them. He had alerted the press in advance. He stepped out onto a balcony to harangue the assembled troops, calling them to reject Japan's American-imposed postwar materialism. You can read Riki Rei's translation of Mishima's speech here.[1]

I don't know how much of his speech Mishima managed to give. His voice was largely drowned out by circling helicopters and the jeering of the troops. But what happened next ensured that many thousands would pore over every word of the written text. Mishima returned to the commander's office, where he and one of his followers, Masakatsu Morita, committed *seppuku*, a form of ritual suicide involving self-disembowelment with a dagger followed by decapitation with a sword wielded by one's second.

Mishima's suicide is often portrayed as motivated by the failure of his attempted "coup." But this is silly. The

---

[1] Yukio Mishima, "A Call to Arms: The Final Speech of Yukio Mishima," trans. Riki Rei, *Counter-Currents*, March 24, 2020.

so-called "coup" was merely a prelude to a suicide that Mishima had been thinking, talking, and writing about—as well as meticulously planning and rehearsing—for years. Mishima's speech and suicide were two acts of a single propaganda drama: first, propaganda of the word, then propaganda of the deed.

What was Mishima's message?

From the start, Japan was a military aristocracy. The highest value was honor. The individual's sense of honor was deeply connected to his national identity, his place in society, and the duties connected with his station. Thus the honor cult upheld the entire social order.

How did one demonstrate the sincerity of one's devotion to honor? By being willing to risk one's life in battle over honor. The samurai preferred death to dishonor. If one is victorious, one can wear one's laurels in good conscience. If one is defeated, one can express one's devotion to honor through suicide.

The samurai's preferred method of suicide is called *seppuku* or *hara-kiri*, which means cutting (*kiri*) the belly (*hara*). The English idiom "spilling your guts" connotes candor and sincerity. The Japanese have a similar idea, which they take quite literally. Mishima wrote that "a person's sincerity is said to be symbolized by his internal organs." To expose one's internal organs shows that you are hiding nothing, holding nothing back. Thus to commit suicide by spilling one's guts is, as Mishima said, a form of "exhibitionistic persuasion."[2]

So what thesis was Mishima arguing for when he plunged a dagger into his abdomen? He wanted to persuade his audience—the soldiers before him, the Japan Self-Defense Force in general, and the Japanese people as

---

[2] Translated and quoted by Andrew Rankin in *Mishima, Aesthetic Terrorist: An Intellectual Portrait* (Honolulu: University of Hawaii Press, 2018), p. 111.

a whole—to turn away from American-imposed materialism and parliamentary democracy and back towards Japan's traditional culture and way of life, the mainstay of which was the aristocratic cult of honor.

Feudalism was abolished in Japan and political sovereignty concentrated in the hands of the Emperor after the Meiji Restoration of 1868. The samurai caste was abolished, but samurai who cooperated with the Restoration were given positions in the new order. In 1873, *seppuku* was abolished as a form of execution, and voluntary acts of *seppuku* became rare. *Seppuku* came to be seen as archaic and transgressive.

However, even after the Meiji Restoration, the militaristic ethos that gave rise to *seppuku* remained powerful in Japan. During the Second World War, countless Japanese longed to prove their devotion to the Emperor by risking death for victory and committing suicide in defeat. The most terrifying expression of this ethos were the *kamikaze* pilots who committed suicide by crashing their airplanes into American warships.

After Japan's surrender in the Second World War, the United States sought to abolish Japanese militarism. The Japanese military was abolished and replaced by the Japan Self-Defense Force, which was little more than a police force and auxiliary of the American military, which guaranteed Japan's external security.

Beyond abolishing the Japanese military, the United States sought to uproot the honor culture that sustained it by making a different part of the human soul sovereign in Japan, namely desire. Post-war Japanese society is highly bourgeois and materialistic, based on the idea that the highest value is a long and comfortable life, to be purchased even at the price of honor.

Aristocratic politics is based on the contrary idea that the highest value is honor, to be purchased even at the price of our lives. The spiritual aristocrat, therefore, must

The Meaning of Mishima's Death

be ready to die; he must conquer his fear of death; he even must come to love death, for his ability to choose death before dishonor is what raises him above being a mere clever animal. It is what makes him a free man, a natural master rather than a natural slave. It is ultimately the foundation of all forms of higher culture, which involve the rejection or subordination and stylization of merely animal desire.

A natural slave is someone who is willing to give up his honor to save his life. Thus modern politics, which exalts the long and prosperous life as the highest value, is a form of spiritual slavery, even if the external controls are merely soft commercial and political incentives rather than chains and cages.

Throughout his writings, Mishima cultivated what can only be called *an erotic relationship to death*. By loving death, he no longer feared it. By ceasing to fear death, Mishima became free to lead his life, to take risks other men would not have taken. He could preserve his honor from the compromises of commerce and politics and the ravages of old age. He could enter and sustain the realm of freedom that is the basis of all high culture. By ceasing to fear death, Mishima struck a death-blow at the foundations of the modern world.

But all that could be dismissed as mere talk until Mishima actually put his words into action.

Did Mishima hope to encourage his followers to commit suicide? Of course not. He even tried to persuade Morita, his second, to live on. He wanted Morita and the rest of the Shield Society—and anyone who cared to imitate them—to prefer death to dishonor, to overcome their fear of death, and then to fight for the restoration of Japanese civilization.

I was once asked, "What is the most honorable form of suicide?" My answer is: "To give up the pursuit of personal happiness and devote one's life to the White Nationalist cause." Mishima's death inspired countless people around the world to similar lifetimes of devotion. We remember his death so that it might inspire similar devotion today.

Counter-Currents, November 25, 2020

INDEX

Numbers in **bold** refer to a whole chapter or section devoted to a particular topic.

A

A Passage to India, 143
abductive reasoning, 92
Abrahamic faiths, 41
accelerationism, 72, 119
Achilles, 117
active imagination, 99
Adler, Mortimer, 105–106
Adonis, 23
Ahab (Captain), 118
Ahasuerus, 25
Alabama, 102, 104, 106
Alasdair MacIntyre, 101–102
alcohol, 33, 141, 169; alcoholism, 37, 111
Allah, 41
Alt-Right, 127, 144
altruism, 2, 7–8
Amerindians, 177
Anderson, Kevin J., 89
Anderson, Lindsay, 135
androids, 21–22, 24–27; see also: replicants
Angry Young Men, 135–36
animals, **21–24**, 28, 178
anti-colonialism, 68
anti-egalitarianism, 68, 185
anti-Semitism, 22, 26, 125, 129

apostasy, 32
arbitrariness, 151–52
archeofuturism, 63, 116, 172–73, 178
archetypes (personalities), 119
aristocracy, 61, 185; Hungarian, 193; military, 197
aristocratic cult of honor, 66; disdain, 66; dynasties, guilds, & initiatic spiritual orders, 91; families, initiatic orders, guilds, & other institutions, 98; forms of government, 66; politics, 198; values, 66
Aristotle, 148, 149n4, 187; *Nicomachean Ethics*, 149n4; *Politics*, 187
Armenian Genocide, 156n7
Armenians, 20
artificial intelligence/AI, **58–62**, 95
Asians, 3, 183
Assman, Jan, 40
Assyrians, 20

Astounding Science Fiction, 69
Atlantis, 179
Atreus, 66
Australia, 177
Austro-Hungarian aristocracy, 193
Avengers, 146
Aztlan, 166, 171, 172

B
banks, 98–99
barbarism, 67, 101
Barclay brothers (Sir David & Sir Frederick), 141
Batman, 147, 151, 156
Baton Rouge, 125
Beati Paoli, 147
beauty, 5, 106, 116–17, 121, 174
Belgium, 30, 40
beta males, 39
Bible, 180
Bildungsroman, 106
biological degeneration, 14
biological race & sex differences, 30, 39, 86
biopolitics, 68
blacks, 40, 55, 124, 129, 173, 177, 183
Blade Runner, **21–25**
body modification, 109
Boethius, 125, 127
Bolsheviks, 146
Boomers, 36, 50, 53
bourgeois, American life, 194; cowards, 31; domesticity, 190; post-war Japanese society, 198; society, 129; values, 67
Bowden, Jonathan, 107, 113, 136n5, 137, 144; *Western Civilization Bites Back*, 136n5
breeders, 190
British Empire, 165
Buffy the Vampire Slayer, 160
bureaucracy, 69, 81, 82, 95, **97–98**, 149, 153–54
Byrne, Bobby, 133

C
California, Northern, 159; Southern, 166
Cameron, James, 43; *True Lies*, 54; *Titanic*, 42
Campbell, John W., 69
Canada, 163, 172
capitalism & capitalists, 41, 43, 52, **54–56**, 109, 177; anti-capitalism, 70
capitalism, 41, 43, 54–55, 70
Catholic Church, 37, 56, 126; Catholicism, 51, 126, 127
Catholics, 129; believing, 45; Irish, 57, 92, 125, 133, 193; traditionalist, 33
Chakravartin, 50

Index

Channel Islands, 141
charismatic leadership, 58
Chinatown (Paris), 37
Chinese, 4
chivalry, 193
Christianity, 2, **5-6**, 15, 16, 22, 27, 38, 40, 41, 169, 173; Gnostic, 28; Orthodox, 35
cigarettes, 33, 37, 136
civilizational cycle, 91, 102
classical republicanism, 187
cloning, 57
Clovis (French king), 35
Coen Brothers, 137; *Blood Simple*, 137; *Fargo*, 137
Cold War, 6, 55
collaboration, 36-39
collectivism, 91
Columbia University, 133
commitment, 37
Communism, 55
community, 13, 16, 101, 107, 111, 175, 185-86; conscious, 164; face-to-face, 175; homogeneous, 170; Jewish, 17, 155; moral, 101; white racialist, 163
compassion, 49
concentration camps, **19-20**
Confederacy, 177
conspiracies, 72, 152
constitution, 149-50, 153
Constitutional Convention, 153

Cosa Nostra, 168
Cossacks, 99
Costello, Jef, 166n7, 183
counter-culture (60s), 68
coup d'état, 32, 150, 154, 196-97
Covington, Harold, 158-74; *A Distant Thunder*, 158, 160-62; *A Mighty Fortress*, 158, 160, 162; *Freedom's Sons*, 158(*); *Northwest Quartet*, 158-75; *The Brigade*, 158, 160, 162; *The Hill of the Ravens*, 158, 161, 162, 171
crime, 1, 3, 5, 6, 34, 75, 109, 138-39, 153, 170, 192
crypsis, 25, 91, 146
cuckservatives, 32
culture of critique, 28
culture, high, 110, 116, 172, 199; junk, 104, 174
cultured thug, 113
cynicism, 37, 60, 63, 67, 82, 119, 193

D

Dalferes, Clayelle, 129
Dark Age (current), 102
Dark Triad, 42, 144; see also: Machiavellianism; sociopaths & sociopathy
Darwinism, 67

David, Larry, 132
De Maistre, Joseph, 45
death, 49, 51, 52, 122, 156; cultivating an erotic relationship with, **196–200**; in *Do Androids Dream of Electric Sheep*, 21, 22, 23, 26; in Houellebecq's novels, 32, 37, 38; in Rand's *Ideal*, 188, 191; in the *Dune* series, 59, 67, 79, 83, 84, 91, 93; in *The Leap!*, 137, 140, 143; in *The Northwest Quartet*, 169, 170
Debussy, Claude, 122
decadence, 30, 43, 47, 101, 107
decency, 4, 42, 174
decision, 2–3, 50, 125, **151–52**, 155
Declaration, 135
deep ecology, 68
Deep Ones, 13–20
Deep State, 120, 121, **153–57**
demographics, 30, 61, 165
demos, 105
determinism, 76, 77
Deverell & Birdsey, 135, 136
Dick, Philip K., 21–29; *Do Androids Dream of Electric Sheep*, 21–28
Dickson, Sam, 165
Dionysus, 23, 82
discretion, 148–49
dishonor, 156, 197, 199; see also: honor
distributism, 30, **185–87**; Catholic, 34
diversity, 3, 11, 87, 90, 110
Docetism, 28
domesticity, 190
Dominican College (New Orleans), 134
drugs, 68, 141, 169, 174
dualism (metaphysical), 65
Dugin, Alexandr, 35
Durocher, Guillaume, 36
duty, 98
dynasties, 35, 91

E

Easter Uprising, 169
Eastern spirituality, 68
ecology, 68
eco-Nazis, 44
eco-terrorists, 51
education, 7, 35, 104–106, 110–11, 115, 118, 121, 164–65, 172, 179; higher, 33, 118; Muslim, 33
egalitarian-populism, 186
Elders of Zion, 146
elites, 60, 110
empathy, **21–25**, 27, **141–42**
epieikeia (equity), 149n4
épuration of the ruling classes, 32
equality, 67, 107, 115, 174; inequality, 116

equity, 149n4
Erdogan, Recip, 154
Esterhazy family, 193
Esther (Queen), 17, 25
estrogen, 96
ethnic cleansing, 32
ethnic mafias, 120
ethnocentrism, 5
ethnonationalism &
   ethnonationalists,
   183, 185
eugenics, 40, 57–58, 64,
   67, 79–80, 86, 92–93,
   178
Europe, 2–3, 7, 30–31, 86,
   115, 177, 186; medieval,
   86, 186
European nationalism, 30
European Union, 31, 141
evil, **5–6**, 9, 14, 32, 42, 52,
   85, 112, 128, 177, 180–81
Evola, Julius, 61, 102, 127
evolution, 64, 67, 92
exception, 148–49, 152
exceptional
   circumstances, 148–
   49, 153

F
facts, 19, 20, 128, 176
family, 34–35, 41, 46, 40,
   53, 68, 80, 90, 92, 102,
   121, 123, 125, 133, 167,
   190, 191
fanaticism, 63, 82, 118, 177
fantasy fiction, 54;
   compared with
   science fiction, 63,
   177–78; see also:
   archeofuturism
fascism & fascists, 40,
   113n1, 130, 172, 194
fashion, 109
Faustian Man, 54–55
Faye, Guillaume, 63, 116;
   Archeofuturism, 63
fear, 4, 8, 31, 52, 93, 104,
   118, 131, 134, 141, 143,
   146, 153; as the main
   motive of liberalism,
   52; of death, 199
feminism, 34, 39, 43, 95,
   108; anti-feminists, 35
feudalism, 56, 66–67, 91,
   198
final judgement, 6
First World, 2, 152
First World War, 165
Founders (American),
   152–53
fraternal orders, 16
freedom, 60, 75, 77–78, 81,
   83, 90, 100, 153, 191,
   199; individual, 52,
   186; religious, 173, 174
Freemasonry, 16, 61;
   Conservative, **61–62**
French New Right, 63
French Quarter (New
   Orleans), 130
French Revolution, 33
French, army, 4, 33;
   history, 6; native, 4,
   16, 33; people, 4, 7, 9,
   33, 39
Führer principle, 168, 173

G

gangsta rap, 40
Garbo, Greta, 189
Gay men, 124, 130–31, 183;
see also: homosexuals
Gelassenheit, 78
General Directorate of Internal Security (French DGSI), 43, 51
genes, 41, 53, 100
genetic engineering, 64, 94
genocide, 5, 20;
Armenian, 156n7
Germany, 20, 193
Gestell, 78
gholas, 65, 67, 72, 94, 100
globalism & globalists, 62, 147
Gnosticism, 28
God, 6, 21, 24, 133, 158, 180
Gogol, Nicolai, 112
Golden Path, **76–79**, 83, 89
golem, 36
Gottlieb, Roger, 123
goyim, 124, 146
Greece (ancient), 115, 117
Greene, Dorian, 130
Greene, Sonia, 17
Guénon, René, 40–41, 45, 61, 102; works: *Initiation & Spiritual Realization*, 41; *Perspectives on Initiation*, 41; *The Crisis of the Modern World*, 102

guerilla warfare, 68, 75, 159, 164, 169
gun porn, 112

H

Haman, 25
Hamas, 159
Hamsun, Knut, 118
Hannukah, 17
hara-kiri, 197
Harrison, John, 85–86
Hawaiians, 166
hegemony, 30, 146
Heidegger, Martin, 43;
Heideggerian ideas, 78, 99
Hepburn, Kate, 194
Herbert, Brian, 89
Herbert, Frank, 54–62, 63–73, 74–89, 90–100, 178; works: *Chapterhouse Dune*, 69, 88, 89, **94–100**; *Children of Dune* (miniseries), 71, 85–86; *Children of Dune* (novel), 60, 71, **74–87**, 88; *Dune* (David Lynch film), 63, **99–100**; *Dune* (novel), 54–58, **60–62**, **63–68**, 69, 74, 85, 88; *Dune Messiah* (miniseries), 71; *Dune Messiah* (novel), 58, **69–73**, 75–76, 85–86, 88; *Dune* universe, 53, 63, 66, 85, 86, 88, 94–95,

91, 99, 178; *God Emperor of Dune*, 58, 69, 74n1, 76n4, **77–87**; *Heretics of Dune*, 57, 59, 69, **94–100**
hereditary monarchies or aristocracies, 56, 61
heredity, 67
heresy, 93
hero-worship, 89
Hezbollah, 159
hierarchy, 64, 97, 138, 149, 195; of command, 168; social, 81, 103
high-trust communities, 39
history, 58, 81, 83, 105, 116, 118; European, 102; French, 6; human, 77, 82, 97, 159; of Duke Leto, 80; of Jewish anti-gentile massacres, 17; philosophy of, 59, 67; Western, 120; world, 12, 159
Hollywood, 26, 163, 194
Holocaust, 26
homelands, 7, 177, 179, 183; white, 110, 156–57, 162, 164, 169–70
homogeneous communities, 39, 170; homelands, 177
homosexuals, 124, 127, 128, 130, 133, 134, 181; see also: gay men; lesbians

honor, 66, 81, 82, 96, 190, **197–99**; see also: dishonor
Hopkins, Bill, **135–45**; *The Leap!*, **135–145**; *The Divine & the Decay*, 135–37; *Time of Totality*, 136
Horne, Lena, 131
Houellebecq, Michel, **30–41, 42–53**; as man of the Right, 30, 43; works: *Annihilation*, **42–53**; *Elementary Particles*, 42; *Serotonin*, 45; *Submission*, **30–41**, 45
Hrotsvitha of Gandersheim, 125, 127
Hugo, Victor, 160
human rights, 136
humanism, egalitarian, 146, 156; liberal, 2
humanitarianism, liberal, 6
Hunter College, 129, 134
Hussein, Saddam, 172
Huysmans, Joris-Karl, 36, 38
hypocrites, 87

I
Ibn Tufayl, 41; *Hayy Ibn Yaqzan*, 41
Ichigaya Barracks, 196
Idaho, 159
Identitarianism, 30, 33, 45, 51, 53

If... (film), 135
Iliad, 181
immigration, 46, 165; see also: migrants
Immortality, 17
India, 1–3, 10, 165; Indians, 3
inferiority complex, 138
initiation, 41, 64
Internet, 95, 175
Iraq, 150, 166
Ireland, 43, 169
Irish Republic, 165
Irish Republican Army (IRA), 168
Islam, 30–32, 35–36, 38–41, 56–57, 184, 186; as masculine & vitalist, 38, 40
Islamists, 153
Israel, 26, 37, 165, 166

J

James, William, 52
Japan, 197–98
Japan Self-Defense Force (the *Jieitai*), 196, 197, 198
Jerusalem, 36
Jesuits, 57, 61, 91
Jesus the Christ, 5, 21, 28
Jewish Journal of Los Angeles, 29
Jewry, 18, 146, 155
Jews, in *A Confederacy of Dunces*, 124–25; in *Adjustment Day*, 180, 183–84; in *Do Androids Dream of Electric Sheep*, 16–18, 21–27; in Herbert's *Dune* series, 99; in Houellebecq's *Submission*, 33, 36; in Perdue's *Morning Crafts*, 105; in the superhero genre, 146, 155–56
Jim Crow, 177
Johnson, Greg, 36n2, 40n3, 61n2–4, 77n9, 86n34, 113n1, 136n5, 139n7, 146n2, 153n5, 156n6,
Judaism, 41
Jünger, Ernst, 176, 181; *Visit to Godenholm*, 176
junk culture, 174
junk food, 174
Jurassic Park, 172, 178
Justice League, 146
justice, 8, **147–49**, 151–52

K

Kaczynski, Ted, 44
Kanakys, 15–16, 20
kamikaze pilots, 198
Kant, Immanuel, 52; *Critique of Judgment*, 52n2; *Critique of Practical Reason*, 52n2; *Critique of Pure Reason*, 52n2
katechon, 6
Kemalism, 153

Kenneth Tynan, 135
Kettle, Ma & Pa, 191
Klein, Jacob, 105
Koran, 40
Ku Klux Klan, 147

L
LARPing, 185
Late Antiquity, 101
Lawrence, D. H., 118
Le Pen, Marine, 30, 32
League of Shadows, 156
Left Hand path, 65
Leftism, 5, 44; Leftists, 2, 4, 8, 12, 34, 39, 45, 55, 109, 126, 185,
Leitmotives, 132
lesbians, 124, 131; see also: homosexuals
Lessing, Doris, 135-36
Lessing, Gotthold, 61-62
Lewis, Wyndham, 188
liberal democracy, 32, 41, 56, 61, 66, 86, 91, 136, 151, 154
liberalism, 5, 43, 52, 66, 152; secular, **5-6**
liberals, 53, 97, **151-53**
Libertarianism, 173
liberty, 98, 173-74
Lincoln, Abraham, 120
Lindsay Anderson, 135
loneliness, 38, 46, 141
Look Back in Anger, 136
Louisiana State University, 123, 125
love, 13, 31, 34, **49-51**, 54, 81, 107, 116, 121, 128, 181, 199
Lovecraft, H. P., 13-20; *The Shadow over Innsmouth*, **13-19**
low church Protestants, 192
Lucas, George, 63
Lynch, Trevor, 21n1, 77n9, 86n34, 146n2; *Return of the Son of Trevor Lynch's CENSORED Guide to the Movies*, 86n4; *Son of Trevor Lynch's White Nationalist Guide to the Movies*, 146n2; *Trevor Lynch's White Nationalist Guide to the Movies*, 21n1, 77n9, 146n2

M
MacDonald, Andrew, 160
MacGibbon & Kee, 135
Machiavellianism, 142, 144, 193; see also: Dark Triad; sociopaths & sociopathy
MacLauchlin, Cory, 124, 125n2, 129n4-5; *Butterfly in the Typewriter: The Tragic Life of John Kennedy Toole & the Remarkable Story of A Confederacy of Dunces*, 124n1, 125n2,

129n4–5
Maenads, 82
mafia, 159
magical universe, 63, 99
Márquez, Gabriel Garcia, 107; *One Hundred Years of Solitude*, 107
marriage, 16–17, 46, 48–49, 70
Marxism, 6; Marxist propaganda, 2
masculinists, 35
masculinity, in Islam, 38, 40; in neo-paganism, 45
Mashita, Kanetoshi, 196
masked vigilante genre, 147
masses, 27, 91, 110, 115
master, natural, 199
McAvoy, James, 86
media, 2, 7, 12, 16, 26–27, 32, 146, 185
medieval Europe, 86, 186
Mediterranean, 3, 10, 143
Meiji Restoration, 198
Melanesia, 15
memory, 65, 74; ancestral, 57–58, 65, 70, 72, 74, 76, 92, 94; android, 21, 24
mentats, 57, 64, 72, 94, 96
Mercerism, 22–28
metapolitics, 12, 39, 61, 119
Mexico, 106, 166
MGTOW (Men Going Their Own Way), 35
middle age, 118

Middle Ages, 133, 147
Middle Easterners, 177
Migrant Crisis of 2015, 7
migrants, 3–4, 7, 9, 22, 43, 45, 164; see also: immigration
military, 8, 10, 130, 155, 172
Minnesota, 122
Mishima, Yukio, **196–200**; as man of the Right, 196
mixed regime, 173
modernity, 41, 52, 101, 105, 127
money-lending, 16
monotheism, 64
Montessori, Maria, 106
moral life, 101
morality, 146
Morita, Masakatsu, 196, 199
Moses, 23, 40
Muhammed, 41
multi-racial coalitions, 183–84
Muslim Brotherhood, 30, 33–34, 36
myths, 21, 167, **176–77**

N
narcissism & narcissists, **126–27**, **137–38**, 141–42, 144, 193
National Front, 30–33, 45
National Rally, 45, 47
National Socialism, 35, 44; American, 160, German, 168, 173

nationalism, 11; ethnic, 61, 86n36; ethno-, 185; European, 30; see also: White Nationalism
nation-state, 62
nature, **23–24**, 41, 44, 47, 59, 95, 97, 104, 114, 172, 174, **177–80**; human, 134
Nazi Germany, 20
Nazis, 3, 147; eco-Nazis, 44
NEETs, 127
neocons, 146
neo-paganism & neo-pagans, 45, 167, 173
networks, 110, 154, 170
New Orleans, 124, 125, 134
New Right, 60, 68, 103, 107, 108, 110
New York City, 131, 163, 184
New Zealand, 177
Nietzscheanism, **137–38**, 140, 142, 194
nihilism, 4, **42–44**, 53; racial, 6
nobility, 42, 86, 91
Nodes, 110
Nolan, Christopher, 77n9, 147, 150; *The Dark Knight*, 77n9, 150; *The Dark Knight Rises*, 147
Non-Governmental Organizations (NGOs), 7, 154
non-whites, 4, 7–8, 12, 31, 36, 108, 109, 120, 162, 163, 165, 170, 183–84
norms, 115, 121
Norse myths, 167

O

O'Connor, Flannery, **132–33**, 192; *Wise Blood*, 192
O'Connor, Frank, 193
O'Meara, James J., 127, 183
O'Meara, Michael, 176n2
O'Reilly, Farnham, **176–82**; *Hyperborean Home*, **176–82**
Office of Special Plans, 146
Oh! Calcutta!, 135
Old Ones, 18, 20
Old Testament, 24, 174
oligarchs & oligarchy, 55, 98, 109, 184
Oliver, Revilo P., 137
Operation Nemesis, 156n7
orders (Jesuit, knightly, monastic, or Sufi), 56, 57, 92, 61
oriental despotism, 94
Orientals, 177
original sin, 6
Osborne, John, 135
Osiris, 23, 59, 84

P

Pacific Northwest, 163–64, 166
paganism, esoteric, 41; neo-, 45, 167, 173

Paglia, Camille, 107;
    Sexual Personae, 107
Palahniuk, Chuck, 183,
    185; *Adjustment Day*,
    183–87; *Fight Club*,
    183n2
Palestine, 159
Panama Canal Zone, 163
paranoia, 123, 128, 133
Passover, 17
patriarchy, 34, 35, 87
Paul, Ron, 35
peace, 36, 64, 69, 81–82,
    110, 130, 159
Peikoff, Leonard, 188
Percy, Walker, 123, 124
Perdue, Tito, **102–105**,
    107, **110–12**, 113, 115,
    122; works: *Cynosura*,
    104; *Fields of
    Asphodel*, 103, 114; *Lee*,
    103, 114; *Love Song of
    the Australopiths*, 114;
    *Materials for All
    Future Historians*, 114;
    Morning Crafts, **104–
    107**, 110, 114;
    *Opportunities in
    Alabama Agriculture*,
    103, 114; *Philip*, 104,
    114; *Reuben*, 103, **113–
    122**; *The Bent
    Pyramid*, 114; *The
    Gizmo*, 114; *The New
    Austerities*, 103, 114;
    The Node, 103, **108–
    112**, 114; *The
    Philatelist*, 114; *The
    Smut Book*, 104, 114;
    *The Sweet-Scented
    Manuscript*, 103, 114;
    *The William's House
    quartet*, 114; *Though
    We Be Dead, Yet Our
    Day Will Come*, 114
Persia, 25
pessimism, 10, 51, 101
philosophy of history,
    Frank Herbert's, 63
Pierce, William, 160; *The
    Turner Diaries*, 160
Plato, 83, 122, 149n4;
    Platonism, 192;
    Republic, 149n4
Pléiade (publisher), 38
political correctness, 29,
    103, 108
political philosophy, 151;
    Frank Herbert's, 54,
    58, 63
pollution, 109
polygamy, 39–40, 186
Pontic Greeks, 20
populism; see:
    egalitarian-populism
pornography, 119, 159
postmodern value
    systems, 116
power, dictatorial, 137;
    executive, 150; in *Do
    Androids Dream of
    Electric Sheep*, 23, 26;
    in Houellebecq, 30,
    32–33, 35, 41, 44, 50–
    51, 56; in Perdue, 110,
    115, 118, **120–22**, 137–

38; in *The Camp of the Saints*, 5, 9, 12; in the *Dune* series, **57–61**, 65–66, 69–73, 77, 83–85, 90–91, 94–95, **97–98**; in *The Leap!*, 144; in *The Shadow over Innsmouth*, 20; in the superhero genre, 149, 154–55, 163, 173; Jewish, 36; political, 72, 114, 122, 186
pragmatism, 16, 58, 168
prescience, 59–60, 65, 69, 71, **73–80**, 85, 89–90, 93, 95, 100; prescient beings, 76; prescient powers, 57, 59, 74
professional wrestling, 120
Project for a New American Century, 146
propaganda, 2, 109, 119, 120, 164, 197
property, 3, 4; private, 81, 186, 187
prosperity, 14, 73, 199
psychoanalysis, 129
Purim, 17
Putin, Vladimir, 35

Q
quantity vs. quality, 117, 119, 173

R
race, 2, 13, 17, 20, 32, 35, 108, 177, 189; human, 43, 58, 59, 67, 76–78, 81, 84, 86, 89–93; race-mixing, 180, 183; race war, 2; races, 159, 174, 177, 179; racism, 5, 7, 14; racist, 40, 44, 167; super-race of elves, 177; white race, 1, 3, 5, 11, 39, 41, 61, 66, 107, 110–11, 159, 166, 172, 176
racial hatred, 177
racial miscegenation, 14
racial nationalist fantasy literature, 176
racism, 5, 7
Ralston, Richard, 188
Rand, Ayn, 142, **188–95**; *Anthem*, 188; *Ayn Rand, Three Plays*, 188; *Ideal* (novel & play): the story critiqued, 189–95; comparison of novel to play, 188, 191, 192, 194; *Ideal: The Novel & the Play*, 188; *The Early Ayn Rand: A Selection from Her Unpublished Fiction*, 188; *We the Living*, 188
Raspail, Jean, **6–12**, 32; *The Camp of the Saints*, **6–12**, 32

Ravel, 122
reason, 52; Aryan, 174; practical reason, 52; theoretical, 52
Rei, Rikki, 196n1
religion, in *The Camp of the Saints*, 2; fundamentalist, 39; in Houellebecq, 34–35, 40, 53; in the *Dune* series, 63–64, 85, 89, 91–92, 99; in the *Northwest Quartet*, 69, 172–73; in *The Shadow Over Innsmouth*, 16, 22; Jewish, 16; Lessing's view, 62; masculine vs. feminine, 38; Mercerism (P. K. Dick), 22–23, 27; Savitri Devi's Esoteric Hitlerism, 44; Traditionalist view, 40–41, 64
Renaissance Fairs, 185
replicants, 22; see also: androids
reproduction, 39, 108
republicanism, classical, 98, 187; French, 31
responsibility, 3, **151–53**, 156
revolution, ethnonationalist, in *Adjustment Day*, 183–85; in Perdue's novels, 114; in the *Northwest Quartet*, 120; invisible, 120; moral, 12; political, 12, 115; radical, 32; Right-wing, 32; sexual, 43
Rhodesia, 4, 163
Right, 8–10, 12, 30–32, 35, 43–44, 48, 54, 67, 144, 196; men of the Right, 9, 43
Rightists, 32, 35, 39, 45; New Rightist, 108
Right-wing, 9, 32, 40, 112, 135, 138, 147
Robin Hood, 147
Rockwell, George Lincoln, 160, 180
Romans (ancient), 150–51
Rosicrucians, 67
Rousseau, Jean-Jacques, 33, 114–15, 192; *Émile*, 114
Ruby Ridge, 167
rules, 147–49 151, 166

S
Saint Paul, 180
samurai caste, 197–98
San Francisco, 21, 25, 26
Sand People, 41
Sandler, David, 29
Sark, 141
Satan, 21
Savitri Devi, **44–45**, 179
Schmitt, Carl, 147–49, 151–54, 156; *Political Theology*, 148n3
Schwarzenegger, Arnold,

Index 215

154
science fiction, 21, 31, 54, 63, 74, 111, 161; compared with fantasy fiction, 63, 177–78
Scott, Ridley, 21
Seattle, 21, 25, 161, 162
secession, **162–63**, 166
Second Anglo-Boer War, 20
Second World War, 102, 198
Seinfeld, 132
self-government, 98
seppuku, 196–98
sex, 25, 30, 37, 39, 49, 50, 86, 94, 124, 129
sexual perversion, 109
sexual promiscuity, 109, 172
sharia, 33; see also: White Sharia
Shield Society (*Tatenokai*), 196, 199
shoggoths, **18–19**
siddhis, 65
Simon & Schuster, 123, 125
slavery & slaves, 22, 94, 98, 105; natural, 199
snuff films, 120
Social Credit, 186n3
social reformers, 87
Social Security, 165
sociopaths & sociopathy, 22, 27, 137, 141, 144, 193–94; see also: Dark Triad;

Machiavellianism
soixante-huitards, 32
South Africa, 106, 166
South America, 177
Southern Gothic, 103
Southwest (USA), 166
sovereign, 148–50, 152–53, 155–57, 198
sovereignty, 147–50, 152–57
Soviet Union, 20, 55
space exploration, 54–55, 81
space travel, 65, 66, 78, 89, 91, 178
Spartans, 150
Spengler, Oswald, 43, 45, 67
St. Benedict, 101, 110
St. John's College, 105–106
Stalin, 193,
Star Wars, 63
Strauss, Leo, 105–106
Stuart Holroyd, 136–36
suicide, 124, 169, 180, 189, 193, **196–99**
superhero genre, 146
superheroes, 146–57
superman (in the *Dune* series), 58, 69, 74, 85, 90, 96
supervillains, 146
swastika, 20
Swift, Jonathan, 123
Switzerland, 4, 99

T
Tantra, 65

Tarantino, Quentin, 160
tarot (in *Dune*), 71
teleportation, 178
Third Reich, 177
Third World, 109; Third Worlders, 4
Thirty Years War, 52
thumos, 81–82, 87, 90
Time of Totality, 136
Tolkien, J. R. R., 45, 177, 178, 181; *The Lord of the Rings*, 181
Toole, John Kennedy, 123–134; *A Confederacy of Dunces*, 123–134; *The Neon Bible*, 133
Toole, Thelma, 124–25, 133
Tradition, 195
Traditionalism & Traditionalists, 30, 35, **40–41**, 61, 64, 67, 102, 105, 176
Tulane University, 133
Turkey, 153–54
Turks, 20

U

Übermensch, 137, 140
Unabomber, 46
United States, 102, 109, **158–59, 162–66**; 172, 185, 198
universal basic income, 186
University of Paris-Sorbonne, 38
University of Southwestern Louisiana, 133

V

values, 33, 41, 98, 191–93; aesthetic, 116; archaic, 63, 178; aristocratic, 66; Christian, 5, 11; Classical, 11; commercial, 66; modern, 147; mundane, 61, 191; natural, 5, 11; Republican, 31; Rightist, 35; transcendent, 35, 38, 191, 199
Vendicatori, 147
Vico, Giambattista, 43, 67
vigilante, 147, 150, 156n7; see also: masked vigilante genre
Virgin Mary, 192
virtues, 133, bourgeois, 67; classical, 168; martial, 67; white, 5
vitalism, 40, 44; & Islam, 40

W

war porn, 159
Warhammer 40k, 54
Washington, D.C., 163
Western civilization, 31, 102–14
Whedon, Joss, 160
white guilt, 2, 5, 8, **11–12**
White Nationalism, 39,

163, **169–70**, 176, 185;
White Nationalists,
35, 41, 61, 111, 154, 156,
162, 184
White Nationalist
revolutionary fiction,
160
white pride, 12
white race, 1, 4, 166, 177
White Sharia, 185–86
Wicca, 51
Wilson, Colin, 135–37, 144;
*The Angry Years: The
Rise & Fall of the
Angry Young Men*,
136n3–4
women, 2, 4, 7, 17, 34, 39,
58, 65, 82, 87, 94, 101,
108, 111, 117, 122, 127,
134, 142, 167, 173, 174

womyn, 39
world history, 12, 159

X
xenophobia, 13
Xenophon, 168
X-Men, 146

Y
Yaitanes, Greg, 86
yoga, 57, 65
youth, 117, 136

Z
Zelensky, Wolodymyr, 46
zensunnis, 72

About the Author

Greg Johnson, Ph.D., is Editor-in-Chief of Counter-Currents Publishing Ltd. and the Counter-Currents.com webzine.

He is the author of twenty-one books (all published by Counter-Currents, unless otherwise noted): *Confessions of a Reluctant Hater* (2010, 2016), *Trevor Lynch's White Nationalist Guide to the Movies* (2012), *New Right vs. Old Right* (2013), *Son of Trevor Lynch's White Nationalist Guide to the Movies* (2015), *Truth, Justice, & a Nice White Country* (2015), *In Defense of Prejudice* (2017), *You Asked for It: Selected Interviews*, vol. 1 (2017), *The White Nationalist Manifesto* (2018), *Toward a New Nationalism* (2019, 2023), *Return of the Son of Trevor Lynch's CENSORED Guide to the Movies* (2019), *From Plato to Postmodernism* (2019), *It's Okay to Be White: The Best of Greg Johnson* (Ministry of Truth, 2020), *Graduate School with Heidegger* (2020), *Here's the Thing: Selected Interviews*, vol. 2 (2020), *Trevor Lynch: Part Four of the Trilogy* (2020), *White Identity Politics* (2020), *The Year America Died* (2021), *Trevor Lynch's Classics of Right-Wing Cinema* (2022), *The Trial of Socrates* (2023), *Against Imperialism* (2023), and the present volume.

He is editor of *North American New Right*, vol. 1 (2012); *North American New Right*, vol. 2 (2017); Julius Evola, *East & West: Comparative Studies in Pursuit of Tradition* (with Collin Cleary, 2018); Francis Parker Yockey, *The Enemy of Europe* (Centennial Edition Publishing, 2022), Alain de Benoist, *Ernst Jünger: Between the Gods & the Titans* (Middle Europe Books, 2022), Francis Parker Yockey, *Imperium: The Philosophy of History and Politics* (Centennial Edition Publishing, 2024), plus works by Savitri Devi, Collin Cleary, Kerry Bolton, and Jonathan Bowden.

www.ingramcontent.com/pod-product-compliance
Lightning Source LLC
Chambersburg PA
CBHW030107170426
43198CB00009B/528